IN THE MIDST OF IT ALL

Christopher L. Price

Copyright © 2019 Christopher L. Price

All rights reserved. No part of this book may be reproduced or transmitted in any form or by any means, electronically or mechanically, including photocopying recording or by any information storage or retrieval system, without permission in writing from the author.

Printed and bound in the United States of America

International Standard Book Number: 978-0-9829776-5-1

Table of Contents

Chapter One 7

Chapter Two 14

Chapter Three 25

Chapter Four 46

Chapter Five... 70

Chapter Six 82

Chapter Seven 96

Chapter Eight 118

Chapter Nine 143

Chapter Ten 171

Chapter Eleven.. 211

Foreword

In the Midst of It All is the third autobiography in the series that began with *I Stood Alone*. As with my previous autobiographies, I took great care to protect the feelings of my family and friends, while maintaining the truthfulness of my journey. My intention in sharing my story was not to maim anyone's character. Instead, I endeavored to convey my personal experiences in a way that readers would be able to fully appreciate the enormity of my tribulations; and, to thereby, recognize the unwavering presence of God as He traveled with me throughout the chaos of my life.

Dedication

This book is dedicated to Lee L Johnson (1933-2007). The lessons you taught me helped to guide my steps; the strength you passed on sustained me.

Life sometimes hurls obstacles in our pathways: events that cannot be foreseen; occurrences that threaten our existence.

Chapter One

The frigid air gushed into the rented minivan as I opened the door. The below-freezing temperatures were not uncommon for that time of the year; yet, the coldness still caught me by surprise. I hurriedly exited the vehicle, stretching my aching muscles the moment my feet landed onto the pavement.

The trip from Atlanta, Georgia to Toledo, Ohio had been a short one. I looked pass my shoulder to my cousin, Brandy. The flat affect of her face conveyed feelings of sullenness. In her resentment, she had driven the entire way to Toledo in virtual silence. She did not utter more than five mumbling sentences to her son, Jared, and me during most of the trip; the exception being when she grumblingly asked Jared what he wanted to eat from one of the many fast food restaurants that we passed en route to Ohio. I unconsciously smirked at her display of righteous indignation. *She'll be all right,* I thought amusedly.

Looking around myself from my position at the side of the minivan, a chill enveloped me that had nothing to do with the air surrounding me. Nothing had physically changed since I was last in Toledo one month ago; however, emotionally and mentally, my world had shifted drastically: Mother, my beloved paternal grandmother, had succumbed to death after battling the ravaging affects of Alzheimer's for the past seven years; Mama, my maternal grandmother, was enthralled in a ferocious fight with pancreatic cancer; I had relinquished my dream-career of acting; my car had been repossessed; and, I was virtually homeless, as I had no home of my own.

I walked to the rear of the minivan to retrieve my luggage. After staggering up the familiar concrete stairs to the green, carpeted porch of Mother's home, I placed my luggage beside the door and rushed back down the stairs.

"Thank you for the ride…I love you," I expressed genuinely to Brandy as I hugged her.

"You welcome, Luda…I love you, too." She replied passionately, hugging me firmly.

What had happened in the few short minutes since we had arrived in Toledo? Brandy had shifted from one mood to another mood as effortlessly as a chameleon changed colors. I internally shrugged my shoulders, placing her peculiar behavior on a shelf in my mind alongside other idiosyncrasies of ours as humans.

I was home in Toledo, again. I sighed miserably. Try as I did to leave the place of my birth, circumstances had always beckoned me back there.

The year was 2009. Exactly seven years and one month ago, I had been released from prison for having committed involuntary manslaughter. Each moment of my incarceration and every day after my release from prison, I had lived with the realization that I had taken someone's life.

The fact had never escaped my thoughts or my spirit. I thought of the life I had taken as though the deceased was a loved one of mine. I had prided myself on being a person of virtue: I was honest and forthright, kind and considerate, loving and nurturing; yet, a person had ceased to exist because of my actions.

Although, I did not know the person whose life I had taken, I had oftentimes wondered what sort of person he would have become. Would he have been a father? Would he have gone to college? Perhaps, he would have been a small business owner meeting the varied needs of the community in which he lived. The potential for his life was endless; though, because of my misdeed, the possibilities of a future for him ended abruptly one early evening on June 3, 1994.

Just as the fact of my action was clear in my spirit and mind, it was also evident in my status in society as an ex-offender. I had been given the label of felon. With the title came difficulty in acquiring employment; as such, simply surviving was nearly impossible. Despite being a fiercely prideful and independent person, indigence had forced me to depend upon my family to meet my basic needs.

~~~~

She lay on the bed with her head tilted upward. Her lips were parted just enough to allow a long transparent tube to fill the opening of her mouth and down her trachea. Beautiful, silver curls of hair were tossed about her head indiscriminately.

I walked closer to the side of the bed. Her body appeared to be twisted in a position of discomfort. She did not look asleep, nor did she look peaceful, as I had heard some people say of those in her condition.

Her oncologist placed her in a drug-induced coma. The nurses assured me that she would not be in the coma for long, only long enough for her body to recover efficiently.

"Mama?" I whispered in her ear.

I had heard that a person in a coma could hear when someone spoke to her. Whether she could hear me or not, I still would have shared my thoughts to her. I needed the reprieve. Talking to Mama, as though she was conscious, made me feel that everything was all right; that I was not talking to a seventy-four year old woman who was battling one of the most vicious cancers known to humankind.

"I love you, grandmamma," I said as I combed the soft strands of her hair with my fingers. "You have got to get better…I miss you…I miss hearing your voice…"

I looked around the room in search of a comb or a brush. Mama was not a vain woman, but she took particular pride in her appearance, especially her hair. Across the room, I located a comb. Walking the few short steps to get it, I returned to her bedside and began to gently comb her hair as I told her all that was going on in my life, just as I had when she was conscious.

I sat at her bedside for several hours before I decided to leave the hospital. It had begun to get late in the evening. I did not want to have to ask anyone to come to the hospital too late at night to take me to Mother's house. It was trying not having transportation of my own, yet I had to deal with it.

I sometimes wondered how different things would have been in my life, if I had stayed in California.

Employment in social services was far more accessible in Southern California than it was in the East. Armed with my associate and bachelor's degrees, within a few short weeks after relocating to Los Angeles from the Bay area, I had gained employment as a health educator to persons living with HIV. However, east of the Mississippi, employment was a rare jewel for an ex-offender.

My artistic career as an actor had begun to move in a promising direction as well. I acquired a well-known agent who was heavily connected in Los Angeles. I began to audition for more roles and my artistic and social networks had grown. The heartbeat of L.A.'s artistic world reverberated with my own.

It was only a matter of time before I would have achieved my goal of being a successful actor.

I inhaled and exhaled deeply.

Turning my head to the left, I glimpsed my grandmother's lifeless body lying on the daunting bed. Machines beeped randomly. I shook the remnants of the previous thoughts from my head, silently chiding myself for thinking selfishly. Yes, I probably still would have had my vehicle and my job, if I had remained in Los Angeles; though, beyond that, there was no certainty of where I would be in life. The world of acting was filled with unknowns. Many people had sojourned to California with hopes of acting on the silver screen, only to find themselves amongst the many whose dreams had been deferred.

Yes, I was where I needed to be; where my spirit had led me—home.

Chapter Two

Prior to moving back to Toledo, I stayed in Atlanta at my daddy's home. During the interim in Atlanta, I had registered to graduate school at Tiffin University in Ohio. I decided that I needed to do something productive with my life while I was in Toledo.

Classes had begun during the second week of January. I was simultaneously excited and nervous. My previous attempts at graduate school did not end very well. I wondered if I would be able to handle the rigors of academia with everything that was going on in my personal life, yet I surmised that I had no other choice but to succeed.

Mama was conscious by the time the school term began; however, she could not walk. Having lain comatose for so long had weakened the muscles in her legs. After thirty gruesome days in a rehabilitation center and hours upon hours of rigorous muscle strengthening exercises, she was finally released to go home.

After Mama's release from the hospital, I decided to move to her home from Mother's house, so that I could spend more time with her as she recovered.

My academic schedule was unyielding. I had opted to pursue my master's degree online. Web-based courses were challenging in their own right. Unlike traditional classes in which students met face-to-face in classrooms several times a week, web-based education utilized online discussion boards to engage students in dialogue and intense writing assignments for instructors to measure students' understanding of the information.

I had also chosen to take the accelerated program, so that I would complete the program in a year's time. My days and nights were consumed with reading scholarly journal articles or writing essays. Despite the constant flow of work to do, I had devised an effective system of juggling my education with my personal life.

Each morning, I awakened early to spend time with Mama and to assist my aunt, Rachel, with whatever help she needed in caring for Mama. Afterward, I would walk to the library to complete my schoolwork. Shortly after dusk, I would return to Mama's house, change into my workout clothes, and ride the bus to the gym to workout for a couple of hours. Returning to Mama's house, she and I would talk for an hour or two before we retired for the evening.

Generally, my days were monotonous; however, there were some days when I had to alter my schedule for my grandmother.

"Christofa," Mama began in her southern tone, "you gone go to the doctor with me, baby?"

"Yes, if that's what you want, Mama. When's your appointment?"

"Rachel, when is my appointment?" Mama would ask in a near whisper. The strength of her voice had not yet returned to its former vitality.

"It's at 9:30, Mama, but, if Chris has schoolwork, it's all right. We'll be fine," Aunt Rachel stated warmly.

I turned to look at Mama. She did not regard the latter part of Rachel's statement. I smiled inwardly. Her love and want of my presence was endearing. I sat my bookbag on the floor as I began to peel off the layers of my winter clothing.

Just as I was about to remove my hat and scarf and after I had shed my winter coat, two sweaters, and winter boots, "Well, baby, if you need to leave, you gone on…," Mama said softly.

I looked down at her incredulously as she sat in her wheelchair, "Lady, please, you know you want me to go with you!" I said with a smile that spread across my face as wide as the seas. She smiled meekly as I kissed her forehead.

~~~

I was lonely. I longed for the joy of experiencing the journey of life with someone; the emotional, mental, and spiritual support; the ease of bearing one's fears, hopes, and dreams of the future.

It had been exactly a year since I had ended my previous romantic relationship with Charleston—the love of my life, at that time. Despite our love of one another, our relationship was tumultuous; dishonesty, arguing, and even fighting had become commonplace.

I had never imagined that I would be in an unhealthy romantic relationship. For as long as I could remember, I had been surrounded by people whose lives were encumbered with dysfunctional relationships. I did not want such a relationship for myself. Yet, despite my earnest of attempts, I always seemed to be entangled in drama-filled relationships.

Perhaps, the issues within the relationships rested on me.

With a fine-toothed comb, I raked over my personality trying to fairly place the shortcomings of the relationships where they belonged. I had absolutely no problem admitting my faults. If the responsibility for the chaos lay on my shoulders, I would have humbly accepted it.

Generally expressing, I was an incredibly loving and supportive person. I honored the sanctity of love. It was my belief that, when God blessed two people with the gift of love, it was their responsibility to treasure, to revere, and to nurture that blessing.

However, in spite of my attributes, I was also impatient, quick-tongued, and, at times, simply mean. The same mouth that effortlessly encouraged and blessed was also capable of verbally maiming anyone whom I perceived as a perpetrator. It took a great deal for me to get upset: the hapless person would have had to have violated me many times over before I unleashed my wrath; though, once it was set free, there was seldom any turning back from my anger.

As I thoroughly examined my flaws, I knew full-well that the issues within my past relationships did not rest solely on me. As valid as were my shortcomings, they were not the cause for the eventual demise of my relationships. Being smart-mouthed and impatient did not cause Charleston to habitually misrepresent the truth, nor did they propel Mally (my lover before Charleston) to flirt and to entertain the advances of someone other than me. No, those dishonors were their personal issues, not mine.

Yet, regardless of where the responsibility for the failures of my former relationships lay, I was still alone. No amount of stone-throwing altered that fact. No blame-casting would ease my yearning of an intimate connection that could be found in a romantic relationship.

~~~~

I had never been content with simply "getting by." Accepting a life of poverty was not an option for me; simply achieving average grades in school was not permissible to me; settling in love was beyond comprehensible to me. I firmly believed that a person should always look for fulfillment wherever, or in whomever, it could be found.

I traveled to Minneapolis, Minnesota in search of him. Sure, I needed a break from the stressfulness of school; and, yes, I wanted to experience a new city in which I had never been; though, the ultimate reason for my excursion was to meet him.

We had cyber-met on a gay chat site in which I had become familiar. I relished our uncomplicated chats, our vibe. In fact, I enjoyed them so much so that I whimsically made travel plans to Minneapolis to visit him. He excitedly welcomed the thought of me visiting and for us to have a face-to-face meeting.

I arrived in Minneapolis on a sunny, winter afternoon. Surprisingly, despite the more than chilly temperatures, the warmth of the city could still be felt. The city was splendid. I had smartly chosen a very chic hotel in Downtown, Minneapolis, so that I could better experience the heartbeat of the city.

He arrived outside of my quaint hotel room late in the evening. I opened the door and there he stood. He was tall: 6'1 and solidly built. I was pleased with what I saw. He looked like his photos: fine, blond hair; soft, blue eyes; and, pale, nearly translucent skin.

I had a great love of Blackness: from our voluptuous, well-sculpted bodies to the many hues of our skin to our command of the arts, athletics, and intellectualism; yet, I still appreciated the beauties of different races. I loved the slants of Asian eyelids fixed firmly on smooth skin and round faces; the mesmerizing dark features of Arabs and Latinos; and, the varied tones of Whites.

The expanse of my mind would not allow me to limit myself to date only one people. The love that I embraced was not, nor could not be confined to one race—or to one gender.

"Hi. My name is Brett." He said in a low, baritone voice as he shook my hand firmly.

I smiled broadly. I liked his voice; its timbre was reminiscent of a Black guy's. His speech, however, was entirely White guy. I liked it. It was sometimes unnerving to me to hear White guys using the vernacular that was typically associated with Black folk or to hear a Black person speaking with the vocal inflections that were usually common in White people's speech.

I could not deny that I was incredibly attracted to him. Aside from his good looks, talking to him was easy. He was intelligent, kind, and a bit goofy. His laughter made me smile: it was quirky, but sincere.

~~~

For a brief moment, our attraction toward one another consumed us. We kissed and rolled around in the bed as we hungrily explored each other's body with our hands. Passion and desire had overpowered us. It did not seem wise to begin a relationship by having sex the first time that we met, yet, under the weight of lust, we were rendered powerless, until, by some found sensibility, Brett had the good judgment to stop us from going any further than we already had.

I surprised myself by kissing Brett. I had never been much of a kisser. Most people had always presumed that I enjoyed kissing or, at the very least, that I would be good at it, because of the fullness of my lips; however, my lips were deceptive. Kissing was not something that I particularly relished, except when kissing involved any one of my past romantic partners. I could kiss them anytime and anywhere, though to casually kiss someone—a date or otherwise—was not me. Though, Brett was different for reasons that were not yet known to me.

After Brett and I had gained control of our inner yearning for one another, we composed ourselves and began a lively conversation for several more hours, until he announced that he had to leave to prepare for work the following morning as a commercial banker. We hugged long and firmly before he exited the room.

I was pleased with Brett. He seemed to be a great guy.

~~~

The next day, Brett and I met for a simple lunch at one of the many eateries in Downtown Minneapolis. As was the case the previous night, we thoroughly enjoyed one another's company. We talked fluidly about our lives: our childhoods, our educations, our past lovers, and our plans for the future. I even learned a fun-fact about Minnesota.

"So, I'm not originally from Minneapolis," Brett stated, casually.

"Oh, no? Where are you from?" I asked.

"Well, I didn't move here until I graduated from college a couple years ago."

"Hmm, okay," I said attentively.

"I'm from a small town called Elbow Lake. It's about three hours west of here, but I can do it in about two! Me and Betsy don't play!" Brett said as he laughed heartily at his reference to how fast he drove his car.

"Well, how big is the town?" I wondered.

"It's about a few hundred people; just slightly more people than there are in St. Olaf," Brett said matter-of-factly.

"St. Olaf?" I exclaimed. "You mean from where Rose Nylund of the sitcom "The Golden Girls" lived?!" I asked astonishingly.

"Mmhmm," he replied affirmatively.

"Oh, my God! I didn't know that St. Olaf was a real city!"

I was bewildered. I assumed it was a fictional place; a product of the writers' imaginations. I had no idea that St. Olaf actually existed.

"Oh, yeah. It's a small town, just outside of Elbow Lake. I used to go there a lot as a kid," Brett shared nonchalantly.

"Unbelievable! You know, as I think about you it, you do remind me of Rose with your blond hair and ditzy moments!" I said jokingly.

"I know! That's what all my friends say, 'Oh, don't mind Brett. He's just having another Rose moment!'" He laughed good-naturedly.

"Oh, I was just joking! I didn't mean it for real!"

He continued to laugh. "Oh, no, it's okay! I do have 'blond' moments!" He laughed graciously.

I laughed with Brett. I really enjoyed being around someone who was comfortable with himself. Brett was able to see the humor in a joke, even when the joke was directed toward him. I liked him.

Chapter Three

The blistering cold weather of Northwest Ohio had won its assault against me. Early one evening, after returning from the library, I fell violently ill. A chill radiated outward from the core of my body to every one of my extremities. Contrary to the clattering of my jaws and the shivering of my legs and arms, I was bathed in sweat from the crown of my head to the soles of my feet; my body alternated between cold chills and feeling as though I was in a dry sauna.

I generally slept nude. I delighted in the feeling of the soft linen against my bare skin. Yet, I did not find such pleasure on that night. I retrieved a pair of long thermal underwear, a jogging suit, a pair of socks, a hat, and I quickly jumped into the bed, pulling the bedspread well over my head, until the warmth of my breath threatened to suffocate me.

I slept in the layers of clothing throughout the evening and into the early morning until the sun had begun to peak over the horizon. My fever had broken. I felt markedly better.

After stripping the sweat-drenched clothes from my body, I showered and dressed for the day.

"Hey, Auntie…Hey, Grandmama." I greeted Aunt Rachel and Mama from the doorwell of the first-floor bedroom that Mama occupied.

"Hi, Chris," Aunt Rachel addressed me with a smile.

"Hey, baby. How you feelin' this mornin'?" Mama asked in concern.

"I feel much better," I said from my position at the entrance of the room. I did not want to enter Mama's bedroom for fear of infecting her with the illness with which I had succumbed, just in case all of it had not subsided. "I think I had a flu bug or something, but I must've sweated it out last night."

"Well, that's good, baby. I'm glad you feelin' better," Mama responded warmly.

"Me, too…I'm about to head to the library to do some schoolwork. I'll be back home this evening."

"You don't think you should rest some more, baby?" Mama asked.

"No, ma'am, I'm okay. I don't want to get behind in my work. I'll be okay. I ate some fruit, and I took an Airborne this morning," I replied.

"Airbo'ne? What's that?" Mama asked.

"It's an effervescent that helps strengthen your immune system."

"Oh, okay, baby," Mama said, looking a bit perplexed by what I said.

"It's just a bunch of vitamins...I love y'all," I said as I grabbed my backpack from off of the floor and hoisted it onto my back.

"Okay, baby. I love you, too, baby. Be careful out there, baby," Mama encouraged.

"Bye-bye, Chris," Aunt Rachel said.

I probably should have rested more before I continued my arduous routine of walking to the library, studying, working out, and returning home, especially with the weather being as severe as it was, but I needed to maintain my focus.

Toledo had been hit by a blizzard. Over fourteen inches of snow had fallen from the ash-gray sky, covering the streets and sidewalks with a thick, white blanket. To make matters worse, the temperature had plummeted to below freezing.

I knew the abrupt shift in the temperature had caused my body to succumb to sickness, though I had no choice but to forge forward with my educational goals, regardless of the treacherous weather.

~~~~

I could not say that I knew she was special when I first saw her; though, I could not quite say that she was not special either. What I could not have known at that time was that she would play a pivotal role in my life for many years to come.

She stood at five feet, four inches tall. An average height for a woman, yet her small-framed body made her appear dainty, fragile in her uniform.

"Christapha, this is LaNeeka. She gone be helping to bathe me," Mama said.

"Okay…Hi, LaNeeka," I said warmly.

"That's my son…I mean, my grandson, Christapha." Mama said to LaNeeka.

During my trip to Minneapolis, LaNeeka had begun helping with Mama's care. In the short three days that I was gone, LaNeeka and Mama had formed an immense bond with one another. I could tell that Mama was fond of LaNeeka by the way she looked and spoke to her. Mama had a gracious attitude toward all of the caretakers that came to her home to assist Aunt Rachel with her care, though she seldom engaged in intense conversation with them—LaNeeka was the exception.

~~~

Mama's health had gotten progressively better; although, per her own request, there were times when she had to be transported to the hospital's emergency room via an ambulance. Yet, despite such random hospital visits, her overall health did not seem to falter. Her voice had returned to its former vitality and her weakened limbs had begun to gain strength. In time, she was able to stand and to walk around her small house with the support of a walker.

Mama was determined to get better. She did not like being dependent upon anyone, particularly her family. Amid body pains and general weakness and fatigue, Mama willed her old body to push a little further in an effort to regain her independence.

~~~

"Hey, Geneva!" I greeted my aunt as I entered Mama's house.

"Hey, Chrissie Boo," Geneva smiled weakly.

"What's wrong?" I asked in concern.

Geneva was my Mymomme's baby sister. She and I were like peanut butter and jelly—inseparable.

She was far more to me than simply an aunt, she was my best friend. My love of her pre-dated my earliest memories. At only thirteen years of age when I was born, Geneva babysat me for days, and sometimes weeks, during Mymomme's party years. As a result of Mymomme's irresponsible behavior, an unbreakable bond had been created between Geneva and I.

"Mmmhmm, I don't know. I just don't feel good; like I got the flu," Geneva replied.

"Hmmm, you may be coming down with what I had. I caught a bug or something, but I feel much better now. Hold on, I'ma give you an Airborne," I said as I continued to take off my boots and coat at the front door.

Hours later, I heard a soft tap at the bedroom door as I napped.

"Come in," I said through my sleep laden voice.

"Boy, you make sure you take yo' naps, don't you?" Geneva asked, smiling as she entered the room.

"Mmmhmm, I need them!" I responded enthusiastically. "I wouldn't be able to make it through the day without a good nap. I feel so exuberant afterwards, like I'm ready for round two of whatever the day brings!" I laughed.

"Hmmm," Geneva replied, thoughtfully.

"What's wrong?" I asked as I scooted backwards on the bed to allow her a place to sit.

"I think I got cancer," Geneva replied matter-of-factly.

"Huh? Why you say that?" I asked confusingly.

"I don't know…I just don't feel good."

"Okay, but why cancer? I mean, why of all things would you think that you have cancer?"

"I don't know. I just got a feelin' I got cancer."

"Hmmm," I said as I pondered Geneva's thoughts. "Did you take the Airborne that I gave you?"

"Yeah, I was gone ask you what the name of that stuff was."

"It's called Airborne. It's just a bunch of different minerals and vitamins to help strengthen your body, so that it can better fight colds and stuff."

"Okay, I'ma have to get me some, 'cause it did help…Just say a prayer for me. Okay, Chrissie Boo?"

"Of course, I will."

"Me and Johnny 'bout to go back to Columbus," Geneva stated.

"Already?"

"Yeah, I just wanted to come up here to see about Ma. I'm ready to go back home now. You know, they startin' already."

By 'they', Geneva was referring to her sisters and brother; by 'starting', she meant that my aunts and uncle had begun bickering with one another. Geneva had a very gentle, sensitive spirit. The least amount of discord made her feel uncomfortable.

"Hmmm, I can imagine."

"I love you, bae," Geneva reached over to hug me before she stood to leave.

"I love you, too. I'll call you in a few, okay?"

"Mmmhmm. Love you," she repeated again before departing from the room.

~~~~

She was gone. I returned home late after an evening of studying at the library to find that she was not there.

"Christapha, can you call Rachel for me, baby?" Mama asked of me in her southern drawl as I entered her house.

"Mmmhmm, yes, I will." I replied as I took off my winter gear at the front door. "What's wrong?"

"I don't know, baby. I ain't seen her for most of the day. I been callin' her, but she ain't returned none of my calls," Mama replied dejectedly.

"Hmmm, okay."

After I had shed the last few layers of my clothing, save my jeans and long-sleeved shirt, I walked over to the phone to call Rachel from the landline. After several rings, the voicemail chimed, instructing me to leave a message. "Mama, you want me to leave a message?"

"Yes, baby…just tell her to call me," Mama said softly.

"Okay…hey, Auntie, this is Chris. I was calling to see if you're okay. Mama asked me to check on you, because she hadn't seen or heard from you. Call when you can. I love you. Bye-bye."

"Maybe she'a call you back…She ain't returned none of my calls," Mama repeated herself.

I could tell that Rachel's absence was distressing for her; yet, I did not know what to say to ease her apprehension.

"She's probably at home asleep. I'll give her a call in the morning when I awaken."

"Okay, C.P.... Thank you, baby," Mama expressed, as I helped her to her bedroom to retire for the night.

~~~~

The following morning, I awakened earlier than usual to check on Mama. After descending the stairs, I looked to my right to see Mymomme asleep on the sofa. I turned to the left of the staircase to enter Mama's bedroom.

"Hey, baby," Mama greeted as soon as I stepped into the bedroom.

"Hey, Grandmama. Why are you awake so early?"

"I don't know...I couldn't sleep."

"You're not in any pain, are you?"

"No, I'm fine, baby. LaWanda been in here seeing about me. Is she still out there?" Mama whispered as she pointed in the direction of the living room where Mymomme was sound asleep.

I nodded my head affirmatively in confusion.

"Will you help me to that potty, baby?" Mama asked, referring to the portable toilet in her bedroom.

"Yes, I will." I replied as I began to help Mama to sit in an upright position and to then transfer her body from the bed to the portable toilet.

"I sure hate that I got to ask this of you, baby. I know the last thing you want to see is yo' old granny's fat ass!" Mama and I laughed at her joke, as she placed her arms firmly around my neck for support.

"Naw, I don't mind helping you; that's why I'm here."

"She act like she don't want to. She so rough with me." Mama whispered in my ear. "That's why I waited for you to wake up. I knew you would be comin' to see about me soon," she continued to whisper.

Mama's love of me and trust that I would always be available to assist her warmed my heart; however, what she expressed about Mymomme's behavior enraged me. I was incensed by her treatment of Mama.

"Now, don't you say nothin' to her C.P... I'm all right," she soothed, apparently seeing the anger in my eyes.

"Okay," I said, looking into Mama's eyes.

It took the ABSOLUTE strength of the Creator for me to honor my pledge to Mama by not saying anything to Mymomme. I loved Mymomme with my whole heart, though I absolutely did not like the way that she behaved sometimes.

~~~

Days had gone by and Rachel still had not returned to care for Mama, nor had she returned any of Mama's phone calls. I was perturbed to express the least, but I kept my thoughts to myself.

Rachel was Mama's primary care-giver. Some twenty years prior, Rachel had earned a degree as a Licensed Practical Nurse. As such, she was the most competent of any of us in my family to meet Mama's varied medical needs. Although she had abdicated her role as a professional nurse many years before, Rachel's care of Mama was astounding: she cleaned and dressed Mama's surgical wound with care and proficiency; she prepared Mama's meals and bathed her with the tenderness of a lioness toward her cubs. Rachel's gentle, quiet patience was nothing short of remarkable.

Sadly, however, Rachel's expert care of Mama had become a source of contention for Mymomme and my uncle, Al. I could not quite understand the reason for Al's negative feelings toward Rachel, though Mymomme's animosity of Rachel was no new phenomenon. From what I was told, ever since they were young children, Mymomme had felt less than wholesome feelings toward Rachel.

In Rachel's absence, Mama's primary care shifted to Mymomme; however, because of whatever evil was going on in her mind and spirit, Mymomme had abandoned Mama, too. As a result of her oldest daughters' desertion and her other daughters' preoccupation with their own lives, Mama's care rested on me.

I had no qualm about caring for Mama. I had cooked, cleaned, and cared for Mother (my paternal grandmother) for years during her battle with Alzheimer's; however, Mama's needs were significantly different than Mother's. I knew nothing about cleaning and dressing Mama's surgical wound. And, while I could have been taught, the persons who were the most proficient in teaching me were nowhere to be found.

I was livid. I had no understanding as to how a woman, who had devoted the bulk of her life to loving and caring for her children and grandchildren, could be virtually deserted by those who presumably loved her.

~~~

Once I had assisted Mama to the portable toilet, I gathered her clean clothing for her to change into after she had taken a shower. While Mama sat on her wheel chair, I placed her shower chair in the bathtub. Just as I had finished getting things in order, Geneva walked into the house. Her presence was beyond a welcome sight; it was God-sent.

After Geneva wheeled Mama into the bathroom, I lifted Mama from her wheelchair and placed her in the shower chair. Together, Geneva and I began the task of bathing Mama.

"I woulda never thought in all my years that any of my grandsons would be giving me a bath. All these girls I got…Mmmm mmm mmm," Mama sighed in disappointment with her daughters for failing her.

"Here," I said, as I grabbed her washcloth. "I'll just lather your towel for you and step out of the bathroom to give you some privacy. Don't worry," I smiled at her. "I won't look at you."

I did not know if it was because of the immense love that I felt for Mama, or if it was simply because of the type of person that I was, however, whatever the source of my action, I did not mind helping Geneva to bathe Mama, in the least. In fact, I felt a great sense of pride in knowing that I could be there for Mama during her time of need. Far too often, I had seen her perform well above and beyond the parameters of a wife, mother, grandmother, and friend. She deserved to be given the same regard that she had bestowed upon others.

When Geneva had finished bathing Mama, she yelled for me to come to place Mama back into her wheelchair. Mama was too heavy for Geneva to lift her alone.

"Thank you, baby." Mama said to me after I had wheeled her into her bedroom.

"You're welcome, Mama," I said as I leaned down to kiss her on the forehead. "Mmmm, your hair smells good! And, your silver curls look beautiful! See, I told you that you should have stopped dyeing your hair years ago. Geneva, look at how pretty her hair looks under the light. See the curls glistening?!" I exclaimed.

"Geneva washed it for me," she smiled appreciatively, as Geneva looked on with pride at her mother's beauty and gracious spirit.

~~~

I sent a mass text message to my family requesting that they assist in Mama's care. It made no sense to me that Mama's care would rest on any one individual, especially with a family as large as mine. Al and I contributed monies toward a nurse's assistant to sit with Mama during the times that Al was away at work and I was at the library doing schoolwork.

Rachel still had not returned, and Mymomme vacillated: at times, she was a great help to Mama; while, at other times, she acted as though Mama was a thorn in her side. She behaved liked she deplored Mama's very existence.

"Baby, I don't want to be left here by myself with her," Mama said in a soft voice as I prepared to leave for the library.

"Huh?"

With my hand still resting on the doorknob of the front door, I turned around and smiled in Mama's direction. I had not fully heard what she said. I had grown accustomed to Mama beckoning me into the house for one reason or another, just as I was about to leave for the day. She seemed to always want me near her.

"I don't want to be here alone with her," she repeated herself, nodding her head in the direction of the staircase.

I released my hand from the doorknob. The smile swiftly fell from my face.

"What did she do?" I asked through narrowed eyelids.

"I don't know what's done got into that girl. She act like she done lost her mind or something. She act one way when everybody here and another way when everybody gone. The other day she came at me talkin' about she tired of me treatin' her like I do. I asked the girl what she was talkin' about, but she just said that I know what she was talkin' about... I don't know what's goin' on with her...She came at me yellin' and actin' like she was gone hit me. I picked up my cane, 'cause I was gone hit her across the head with it, if she woulda came any closer at me."

As angry as I was, Mama's last statement that she would have hit Mymomme humored me. I absolutely loved Mama's strength and courage. She reminded me of Sophia, the character Oprah Winfrey portrayed in *The Color Purple*.

I had always been amazed by Mama's valor. Despite being wheelchair bound and recovering from the devastating effects of pancreatic cancer, she still exemplified the courage of David.

My humor at Mama's statement did not last long, however. Just after she finished her sentence, I heard the stairs creak as Mymomme descended them.

"What did you say to Mama?" I asked, trying as best I could to contain my anger.

"What? What you talkin' about?" Mymomme asked innocently.

"Mama said that you approached her as though you were about to hit her and that you was sayin' something about you tired of her treating you like she does!"

"I didn't do that!" Mymomme responded in a surprised tone.

"Yes, you did, Lawanda." Mama said softly as she sat in her rocking chair looking down at the floor.

"Mama, I wasn't gone hit you!" Mymomme said vehemently.

"Lawanda, I don't know what you was gone do. You came at me waving yo' fist and yellin' at me about what I did to you," Mama said slowly, gently.

"If you are so upset with her, why don't you leave her house?! Why stay with someone that you don't like?!" I had begun to lose control of my temper. "I don't understand this, y'all running around treating this woman like she's done something to y'all! She is the same woman who supported y'all when every last one of y'all was on drugs!" I said to Mymomme, regarding her and her siblings' substance use. "She is the same mother that took care of y'all kids when y'all wasn't thinkin' about us, and here y'all are treatin' her like she's committed some great sin against y'all, while y'all praisin' Allen, like he was a god or somethin'! And, she is the same mother who was standing behind y'all when he was calling all of y'all buttholes!"

I was outraged. *What kind of people abandoned their ill mother?!*

I did not know Mama's entire history with her seven children, but I had lived long enough and had heard enough stories to know that she was a great mother to them by anyone's standard. Her children had shared with me how well she dressed them, that their home was always clean, that she cooked breakfast, lunch, and dinner for them when they were in elementary, and how she had tried to defend them against their father during his many abusive rages.

"This between me and Mama. She know what she did!" Mymomme exclaimed.

"No, I don't know, Lawanda. I asked you what I did to you to make you so upset with me, but you wouldn't tell me," Mama interjected softly.

"Whatever she did to you, it can't be no worse than what Allen did to you! I saw him beat you with a brass ashtray and here you are talkin' about 'my dad this and my dad that' like he was the greatest father on Earth! Something is wrong with you and your sisters!

This woman ain't did nothin' to none of y'all, but all of y'all, except for Geneva, actin' like she was some horrible person to y'all!"

"See, what you did?!" Mymomme sneered at Mama. "You done turned my son against me!"

"I didn't do nothin', Lawanda," Mama said calmly.

"She didn't do this, Mymomme! You did this! You hollerin' and standing in her face waving your fist as though you're going to hit her! You act like you don't hear her when she calls your name for help! This is absolutely crazy!" I said exasperatedly. "Again, you need to leave her house and move into your own place, if you don't like her! And, Mama, you need to put her out," I said, turning toward Mama. "I know she's your daughter, but you don't have to accept this stuff in your own house."

"Well, that's what I'm gone do!" Mymomme responded scornfully, as she quickly exited the house.

"And, that's exactly what you should do!" I retorted tauntingly.

I knew that I teetered on the line of respect and disrespect toward Mymomme. In someone's eyes, I may have crossed the line into disrespect long ago, but I did not care if I had behaved disrespectfully. I had lost sight of Mymomme as my mother. I had no idea who the woman was that had stood before me. For the first time in my life, I was ashamed of her. I would have never thought that she would treat Mama as callously and meanly as she did. She behaved like a bully toward an incapacitated woman who happened to be her own mother! A woman that was not only wheelchair-bound, but who was also seventy-four years old and who had undergone major surgery to rid her body of cancer. I was heartbroken.

I genuinely loved Mymomme. She had given me the foundation on which many of my values rested. As a young child, it was Mymomme who taught me to be polite and to treat everyone with respect, regardless of their personal circumstances. My meticulous-nature and strength of character were instructed to me by Mymomme. The virtues in which I governed my life had begun with her.

Where was the mother who I had revered as a child? Where was the woman who had helped to mold and shape me into a loving and thoughtful man? It seemed that woman was gone.

Chapter Four

Tragedy waits for no one. Sometimes, it takes years for misfortune to rear its head; other times, life hurls blow after blow after blow.

"Chrissie Boo, the doctor said I got leukemia," Geneva said into the phone receiver from her hometown in Columbus, Ohio.

"What?!" I replied disbelievingly.

"Mmmhmm, that's the same disease Ray got. I'on want to go through what he did." Geneva said softly as she thought of her brother-in-law's bout with the ferocious disease.

Chemotherapy had so altered Uncle Ray's appearance that upon my release from prison, I did not immediately recognize him. His pecan brown skin color had been charred to an ashen black; his vision had become impaired; and, perhaps most frightening to Geneva, chemo had taken Uncle Ray's once full-head of hair, leaving a scalp of cabbage patches in its wake.

"You may not have to experience what Uncle Ray went through," I encouraged. "What is your doctor saying?"

"Hmmm…I have to go back to see him, but I know he want to test my sisters and Al to see who a match for bone marrow. And, I gotta start chemo," Geneva replied, as she considered the doctor's prognosis.

~~~~

I saw the flashing red and white lights long before I reached the street where Mama's small brick house sat. The rhythm of my heart quickened as I trudged through the mounds of snow. My toes had begun to numb as the snow found its way through the top of my boots, melting as it reached my feet. I attempted to wiggle my toes to ascertain whether they were severely frostbitten, though my efforts were in vain. They were so numb that I could not feel whether I was moving them.

What if I had to have my toes surgically removed? I wondered dramatically as I rounded the corner of the street where Mama lived.

The possibility of my toes being frostbitten slid from my thoughts as I walked up the two short stairs of the front porch of Mama's house. The front door was ajar, revealing a large gurney on which Mama lay.

"Hey, grandmamma," I greeted as soon as I opened the screen door, stepping into the living room.

"Hey, baby," Mama smiled at me.

"What's wrong?" I asked Mama.

"Awww, I just don't feel up to par, baby," Mama responded softly.

"Ms. Randle told me she wasn't feeling good. I asked her if she wanted me to call the ambulance and she told me yeah," Winona replied, the nurse's assistant that Uncle Al and I had retained to be with Mama.

I nodded my head affirmatively in Winona's direction in recognition of what she had shared with me. I liked Winona. She and Uncle Al had been dating for several months. Her relationship with Uncle Al helped to ease my concerns about her care of Mama. Far too often, I had heard of medical practitioners mistreating patients. Not only was Winona a kind woman, but the depth of her love for Al ensured that she would take great care of my grandmother.

"Ms. Randle," the paramedic leaned down to speak to Mama. "We're going to transport you to the hospital now, okay?"

"Yes," Mama replied.

She looked so sweet as she lay on the gurney. She had always been a loving woman. Like most matriarchs in Black families, she had a formidable strength and sternness about herself that accompanied her role as the queen of her household. Cancer, however, had robbed Mama of her stout frame and authoritative demeanor. Lying on the gurney, she looked more like a picturesque, small-bodied, silver-haired grandmother who baked cookies and pies and knitted boobies for her grandchildren—a stark contrast from the woman who had helped to raise me.

~~~

I accompanied Mama to the hospital in the ambulance. Over the next several days, I would awaken early in the morning, get dressed, and drive to the hospital to visit with her before I would go the library to do schoolwork.

I was still without my own transportation; however, Geneva had allowed me to borrow her car while she battled the debilitating effects of chemotherapy. Having transportation again made traversing to and from the hospital, library, and gym far easier than walking through snow and ice.

Mama's stay in the hospital was longer than it had been in the past. Generally, she was only admitted for a day or two and then released to return home. Despite her visit to the hospital having already exceeded three days, she appeared to be progressing well. She had begun to eat more, her speech and general cognitive abilities had continued to improve, and, with the help of a physical therapist, she had gained more strength in her arms and legs, which aided in her mobility.

After Mama's admittance into the hospital, I moved out of her house and into Mother's home. In Mama's absence, I had come to the realization that it was best that I not live there. I could not live under the same roof as Mymomme, knowing that she had mistreated Mama.

For as long as I could remember, Mymomme had always acted nastily toward various individuals for one reason or another; though, she had never consistently behaved meanly toward anyone. Her past acts of meanness were random, and based purely upon her mood at the time. Yet, during a time when Mama was most vulnerable, her behavior was constant. She behaved as though she was possessed by demons.

Although Mama received scattered visits from our family, she did not have a huge outpouring of love and support from our family as a whole. Generally, the same people visited with her day in and day out.

While Aunt Rachel still had not surfaced, her children whom visited with Mama regularly informed Mama that Aunt Rachel had been stricken with a cold or the flu. The illness, however, did not explain why she did not accept nor return Mama's phone calls.

Every morning before I went to the library to do schoolwork and each evening when I returned from the library, Mama would begin our visit together with the same drill:

"Baby, can you call Rachel for me? I still ain't seen her…baby, have you seen Terri? Baby, have you seen Kim?" She asked sadly in reference to her daughters.

Mymmomme and my aunts' near-desertion of Mama pained her to the point of depression. Outwardly, Mama seemed to be doing well, though inwardly she was dying.

I needed a break from everything!

I could not handle entering Mama's hospital room one more day and seeing the sadness in her eyes or hearing the hurt in her voice.

School was beyond demanding. Taking an overload of classes was proving more than I could bear. My grades had begun to falter in statistics; so, in addition to the hours I delegated to studying in the library to complete my assignments, I had to make time to meet with a tutor every day to achieve a passing grade in the class.

Although I continued my usual workout regimen to maintain my emotional, mental, and physical well-being, I still felt scattered. I needed to get away—and soon.

On a whim, I hastily made arrangements to travel to Minneapolis. I bought a cheap ticket to Chicago for one dollar through a new bus company, and I happened upon an inexpensive flight from Chicago to Minneapolis.

Brett and I had remained in contact religiously through text messaging and random phone calls, so that meeting one another again for the second time was as natural as brushing one's teeth after waking in the morning.

We both reveled in the joy of being in each other's company, and I basked in the sheer beauty of Minneapolis during the spring season.

After two days, I returned home to Toledo. Although short in time, the break was exactly what I needed. I felt more at peace in my spirit; as though, I was able to weather whatever life hurled at me next.

"Hey, grandmama!" I beamed as soon as I entered her hospital room.

"Hey, baby," Mama smiled broadly. I walked over to the hospital bed to kiss her on the forehead.

"What you been up to since I been gone?" I asked Mama as I gently touched the soft curls of her hair before I sat down in the large vinyl-covered chair in the room.

"Nothin, baby," she replied sweetly.

Although I had called to check-in with Mama several times a day while I was in Minneapolis, I still wanted to know if anything had transpired that she wanted to share with me in person. Sometimes, there were things that she did not feel comfortable expressing over the phone, particularly if she had visitors.

"Hmmm, okay," I stated thoughtfully. "Has your health impr…"

A knock was heard at the door.

"Hi. I'm Emma, Ms. Randle's physical therapist. You must be Ms. Randle's son…the resemblance is uncanny!" Emma greeted as she entered the room.

Emma was a middle-aged White woman with fiery, red hair and the warm spirit of a southern belle.

I laughed as Mama smiled on pleasingly. "No, I'm her grandson. My name is Christopher."

"Well, no one would ever know it! And, that smile! You definitely inherited your beautiful smile from her!" Ms. Emma said enthusiastically.

"Thank you," I smiled in appreciation of the compliment.

"You're very welcome! And, you'll be pleased to know that Ms. Randle is improving remarkably! Ms. Randle walked all the way around the bed unassisted, and she is now able to lift heavier weights!" Ms. Emma beamed.

"Wow! Good for you, Grandmama!" I said, proudly. Mama lowered her head in humility.

"Yes, indeed. Ms. Randle is improving wonderfully… I'm just going to walk over here to jot down your vitals, Ms. Randle. I forgot to write them down this morning when I was in here," Ms. Emma stated as she walked to the right of Mama's bed.

"Okay," Mama replied softly.

"And, that's it! Thank you, ma'am!" Ms. Emma declared after writing the last of her notes onto a pad.

"You're welcome."

It was endearing to watch and to listen to Mama's rapport with the hospital staff. Mama's quiet nature would leave one to believe that she was timid, however, those who knew her when she was healthy, knew that she was far from shy. Cancer had confiscated the out-going and vivacious woman that I knew and loved.

"It was great meeting you, Christopher!" Emma chirped.

"The pleasure was all mine," I replied, thankful for the favor and care that I witnessed being shown to my grandmother.

"I'll see you on Wednesday, Ms. Randle," Emma stated before exiting the room.

After Emma left, Mama turned her head in my direction to speak to me, "Baby, when you coming back home?"

"Mmmmmn, Mama. I don't know…I don't know if I can live back in your house with Mymomme there. I don't like the way she treats you," I replied, gently.

"Okay, baby," Mama said softly, seemingly accepting with ease my choice not to move back into her home.

~~~~

"You heard about Mama?" Mymomme asked in her heavy, gruff voice.

Although I still felt negatively toward Mymomme for her treatment of Mama, we remained in communication with one another; albeit strained.

"No. What happened?"

"She in a coma," Mymomme replied flatly.

"Okay. I'm on the way to the hospital," I said into the receiver before I disconnected the call.

I did not know what to make of Mama's condition. A coma? How? What had occurred in the few short hours since I had seen her that morning?

I drove in stunned silence to Toledo from Bowling Green State University where I studied.

By the time that I arrived at the hospital, most of my family members were already there in the visiting room waiting to hear the details of Mama's condition from the doctor.

Tension was high. I looked around at the faces of my family. I was pleased with the support that was shown toward Mama. *This is what Mama wanted all along,* I thought sadly.

I saw Geneva in the distance. I hugged various family members as I walked in the direction of where she stood.

Geneva had lost more weight since the last time I saw her, only a couple of weeks prior. She no longer donned a curvaceous figure; a fact accentuated by her form-fitting jeans and over-sized jacket. Her thin frame was uncommon to me; something that I had never known to exist during my lifetime.

"Hey, bae," I said as I embraced her firmly.

"Hey, Chrissie Boo," Geneva responded.

I disengaged from our hug. As I did so, I looked into her eyes. What I saw in them startled me.

Oh, no! She was slipping into a mental breakdown. The latest crisis in Mama's health was more than she could handle, especially with her own physical well-being dangling so precariously.

"How you feeling?" I asked gently.

"I'm okay," Geneva replied uneasily, unconsciously smoothing the edges of her wig with her hand.

Chemotherapy was victorious in its battle against Geneva's once rich, black hair. Strands of fine hair lay scattered about her scalp where soft, curly hair once existed.

"I'on know why they up here…they wasn't around when Mama needed 'em." Geneva hollered vehemently seemingly to no one in particular, though she looked in the direction of India, my cousin's former girlfriend and mother of his son.

"We can be up here," India shouted across the hall. "You ain't the only one that love Ms. Randle!"

"Then, y'all shoulda been coming to visit her, if y'all loved her so much!" Geneva shouted back toward India.

"She get on my nerves… act like can't nobody else be up here, but her!" India said loudly as several of my family members escorted her to another area of the hospital.

"That's why Deandre don't want you…don't know how to talk to nobody!" Geneva hissed in reference to my cousin's decision not to marry India.

Unbeknownst to me, I had walked into the visitor's area at the end of a heated exchange between Geneva and India. The fiasco had become so unruly that the hospital's security had threatened to remove them from the premises.

I truly did not know that families actually behaved as my family did during times of sorrow. I assumed that such behavior was a concoction of directors' imaginations and reserved only for television and film; however, I was clearly wrong.

I was further shocked that India spoke so disrespectfully toward Geneva. Although India and my cousin had never married, Geneva was still her elder. Though, no one admonished India's conduct, so I presumed that blatant disrespect of our elders was yet another one of the many things that had changed during my incarceration.

Just as things had begun to settle with Geneva and India, Mama's primary physician entered the room.

"Hi, folks," the tall, dark-haired doctor spoke from the center of the room. "As you know, Ms. Randle is in a coma. She suffered an aneurism, which has caused blood to form on the brain. There is a possibility that she can come out of the coma; however, she will not be the woman that you knew," the doctor shared in a crisp, professional manner.

"What will she be like?" One of my family members asked from the other side of the room.

"Well, she'll be in a vegetative state. She won't be able to speak or do normal things for herself. We can drain the blood, but, when blood rests on the brain, it deadens it."

"Can she breathe by herself?" Someone else asked.

"Right now, we have her on life support. If she is taken off of life support, she won't be able to maintain breathing on her own."

"What caused the aneurism?"

"We prescribed blood thinners to prevent any blood clots from forming. In cases such as Ms. Randle's, blood clots are very common. Unfortunately, a side effect of using the medication is that it makes the patient more susceptible to hemorrhaging of the brain."

The doctor looked around at our attentive faces as the news of Mama's prognosis registered within our minds.

"Are there any more questions?" He asked, looking around the room. After no one responded, "the decision of what to do, at this point, rests with you."

By decision, the doctor meant that we had to decide whether we would allow him to operate to release the blood that had settled on a portion of Mama's brain or to remove her from life support. The general consensus was that Mama would not want to be in a vegetative state. I personally knew how difficult it was for Mama to depend on us in her previous condition. Having to depend on us for her very sustenance would literally kill her.

While my family talked amongst themselves, I took the opportunity to walk to the room where Mama lay. As I passed the nurses' station, two of the nurses looked at me peculiarly. I was not sure what to make of their look. I could not say that they looked at me meanly; however, the look was not pleasant either. Perhaps, they had heard the commotion that Geneva and India had caused and, as a result, they thought negatively of my family as a whole.

I entered the small room adjacent from the nurses' station.

It was a though I was experiencing déjà vu: Mama lay motionlessly as tubes filled her orifice; machines were dispersed around the bed. I slowly walked to the bed. It was hard to believe that just a few short hours ago the woman lying on the bed was smiling…talking…walking.

"Hi, grandmama…It's me, Chris…I love you," I said, gently touching her hand. I paused a moment as I gathered my thoughts, "well, it looks like this is goodbye."

I began to lower my head forlornly as I continued to ponder the gravity of my grandmother's situation; yet, as I did so, the right side of Mama's body moved. It looked as though she was trying to raise herself from the bed or to reach for something. The movement surprised me. Had it been a twitch I would have disregarded it as an involuntary action of the muscles, however the movement was so exaggerated that I felt that it was voluntary, intentional.

"Grandmama, can you hear me?" I waited for her to move again, though I saw no movement. "Grandmama, make another movement, if you can hear me," I repeated. Yet, again, she did not move.

I tried to dismiss the action as a figment of my imagination; however, I could not. I knew what I saw. Whether the movement was intentional or not, I could not decipher, though I knew she had moved. I thought back to the doctor's behavior as he shared with my family and me the information of Mama's condition. He seemed detached, as though he did not care about the current circumstances of Mama's health.

At the time, I had regarded his demeanor as professional, albeit emotionally removed. I attributed his choice of words and the tone in which he spoke to us as indicative of his professionalism as a doctor; after all, he encountered death and grieving families regularly.

In order to perform his work effectively, he had to maintain a certain level of emotional detachment from his patients and their families, or else the grief of death would consume him, I assumed. However, as I mentally reviewed his behavior, the way that the nurses had looked at me as I passed them to enter Mama's room, and Mama's erratic movement, I wondered if something was amiss.

I shook my head from right to left in dismissal of my thoughts. Perhaps I had read too many of Michael Crichton's novels involving medical malpractice.

I looked down at my watch. Several minutes had gone by since I had been in the room with Mama. I did not want to monopolize too much time with her when many of my other family members wanted to see her as well.

"I love you with my whole heart, grandmamma," I expressed, leaning down to kiss her on her forehead.

~~~

"Hello…Chris?" Mymomme asked into the phone receiver.

"Hmmm?" I responded as I busied myself around Mama's house.

"Mama's gone."

"Okay," I said calmly into the phone.

"You okay?" She asked.

"Yes, I'm fine."

I knew the phone call was coming. I felt the loss of Mama in my spirit long before I received the call from Mymomme.

Moments prior, I had been singing, "His Eye is on the Sparrow." It was one of my favorite songs. As I walked around the house singing, I suddenly felt a tug in my abdomen. I began to sing louder, with more ferocity. Without warning, tears fell from my eyes. It was then that I knew Mama had transcended the earthy realm.

~~~

Mama's funeral was held on May 15, 2009, exactly one week after her death. She looked beautiful as she lay in the canary yellow, rhinestone-studded suit that she was to wear on her seventy-fifth birthday just three weeks away.

In the aftermath of Mama's passing, pandemonium ran amok. My aunts and uncle turned against one another. Though, surprisingly, however, Mymomme remained separate of the chaos that ensued between her siblings.

As was the case with many families after a death, money was the underlying issue. Mama's will stated that her home was to be left to her oldest and youngest children: Rachel and Al. Ironically, on two separate occasions, just days before Mama had succumbed, she asked my opinion on the matter.

"Baby, you know, I left my house to Rachel and Al when I die…but I don't know if I shoulda done that…what you think, baby?"

"Well, why'd you leave it to only them, Mama?" I asked, trying to understand the reason for her decision.

"I don't know, baby," she responded, looking away.

"Well, Mama, you have seven kids…you can't leave something to two of them and not think of the other five," I stated, gently.

"I know, baby…I just didn't want to bother with all that mess. You know, I made Blossom executa' of my estate?" She asked in reference to Rachel's daughter-in-law.

"Yes, you told me."

"I just know those kids of mine gone act a damn fool when I leave here…" Mama expressed prophetically.

True to her words, her children behaved unbelievingly immature. I busied myself with school and working-out, as I wanted no parts of the mayhem.

~~~~

The days, weeks, and months after Mama's death moved along monotonously. My greatest fear laid in being unable to complete my studies, because of the grief of losing Mama. Generally, I faced all of life's challenges directly; however, I had never lost someone as near and dear to my heart as Mama. I did not want to risk falling into a deep depression and not fulfilling my educational endeavor; and, so, I, uncharacteristically, blocked Mama's demise from my consciousness in an effort to complete my degree.

Every day I kept my mind occupied with a consistent routine of waking in the wee hours of the morning to complete my schoolwork until the early evening. I returned Geneva's car to her after she had finished her first round of chemotherapy. Without any transportation of my own, I walked a mile to catch the bus to the gym every evening after I finished studying for the day. I completed the same routine six days a week, giving myself one day to rest and regroup.

~~~~

My long-distance relationship with Brett had come to an abrupt end on June 25. Brett was truly a great guy: responsible, funny, goal-driven, and handsome. While, overall, he had a very pleasant disposition, there were many times when he was ill-tempered and moody.

Try as I did, I could not understand his foul temperament: he had a great job in finance; he had been raised in a balanced, functional two-parent home; he had never known poverty or the damaging effects of it; all of his needs and the vast majority of his wants were met; and, yet, his attitude was sometimes loathsome.

Brett's foul disposition was akin to many Black persons whom I knew, except Brett was not Black. He had never known the wounds of racism, the sting of discrimination, or the degradation of living in poverty, yet he behaved as though he carried the scorn of the world on his shoulders.

I could not or, rather, I chose not to tolerate his behavior. Every single day for at least the past fifteen years, I had been greeted with unfathomable stressors, yet no one suffered the effects of my tumultuous life. I made certain not to allow any of what I experienced to be displaced onto an innocent person whom had nothing to do with my issues. If I could trudge through life with a smile on my face and my head held high In the Midst of It All, then, so, too, could Brett.

Eventually, after four arduous months of maintaining a death-defying routine, I completed the summer quarter of school with a perfect grade point of average of 4.0; however, the joy of having performed so well in school was short lived.

After the summer quarter ended, we students were given a two-week break before the fall quarter began. Without the rigors of school, my mind relaxed enough to absorb the enormity of the loss of my grandmother.

I mentally replayed the last few months leading to Mama's demise.

In my mind's eye, I saw when she was wheeled into the visitor's room before her surgery; tears streaming from her eyes as she looked at our family with love and gratitude. I recalled the weeks of her being in a drug-induced coma; her life-less body attached to various machines for support. I remembered the final days of her life: the vivid sadness in her eyes.

'Baby, you gone come back home?' Remnants of Mama's voice echoed in my ears.

In my naiveté, I did not understand the depth of her question. She did not merely want me at her home, she needed me there. All of her children had abandoned her in one way or another, except Geneva, who, despite battling cancer herself, made certain to support her mother. *In whom else could she turn?* I was the last person in whom Mama felt that she could depend; though, in the end, I, too, had failed her. Under the weight of depression, it appeared that Mama's body had relinquished its fight to live.

Chapter Five

The year 2010 had arrived. In spite of the loss of my grandmother, I completed the last quarter of coursework to achieve a master's degree in criminal justice with a cumulative grade point average of 3.6. Yet, in spite of my educational achievement, the possibility of me working within the field of criminal justice was limited.

Three months before I was scheduled to graduate, I filed a motion with the Toledo Common Pleas Court to have the felony conviction of involuntary manslaughter expunged from my criminal record. However, during the hearing, the presiding judge informed me that the felony could not be expunged, as not all offenses are removable, specifically violent offenses.

It was my hope to gain employment as a counselor within prisons; however, with a felony conviction on my record, there was little to no chance that I would be hired within the penal system. I felt dejected, to express the least. My own experiences with the judicial and penal systems, in conjunction with my education, would have given me the opportunity to positively influence the lives of countless inmates and, ultimately, society as a whole.

~~~

Once again, my plans for the future were thwarted. Though, rather than to dwell on the disappointment of not being able to acquire gainful employment within my chosen field, I began to work on completing my autobiography.

I traveled to Atlanta to spend the first few weeks of the New Year with my father; however, a few weeks quickly rolled into several months.

I did not know what unseen forces had drawn me to Georgia, though I had always felt a sense of peace while I was there.

Basking in the glory of an inner serenity, I continued to write my autobiography. Throughout the day and well into night, I tirelessly hacked away on the keyboard of my laptop, until, on June 16, I had finally fulfilled the Creator's instruction to me nearly twenty years prior, 'Tell your story!'

~~~

The bus ride to Columbus, Ohio was long and arduous; yet, I needed to see Geneva. Although we remained in constant contact while I was writing my autobiography, we had not seen one another in a couple of months.

A week after my visit, I made the trek back to Atlanta to begin the rigorous business of publishing my autobiography.

The phone call came in just as I had finished editing *I Stood Alone*, the title I had given my autobiography. I should have anticipated the call; after all, we had spoken at length many times about the devastation of living with leukemia. Though, no amount of conversations could have prepared me for her words.

"Chrissie Boo, I'ma stop takin' my medicine…" The words oozed calmly from Geneva's mouth.

"Hmmmm," I responded thoughtfully as I tried to weigh the consequences of her words.

"I'm just tired, Chrissie Boo…" Geneva continued.

"I know you are," I replied, understandingly.

"…I don't like taking this medicine…I'm tired of wakin' up and throwin' up…I'm tired of makin' myself eat…I'm just ready to go…And, you know, I know what's it's like up there," Geneva stated, loosely referencing her experience of Heaven.

Years before, when I was only a child of four or five, Geneva had attempted suicide by swallowing a lethal dosage of sleeping pills. Mymomme found Geneva's languid body and rushed her to the hospital where the medical staff pumped the pills from her stomach. However, during the interim, Geneva shared with me that she had died and visited Heaven.

She recalled with absolute clarity the beauty of Heaven and the glory of God. She pleaded with the Maker to allow her to stay in Heaven, but He told her that it was not yet time for her to die. Reluctantly, she re-entered her body; yet, she had never forgotten her experience with death, Heaven, and God.

Though, she loved her earthly family, she longed to return home to Heaven.

"Yes, I know," I said to Geneva as the enormity of her decision trickled into my consciousness.

~~~

The task of publishing my book was cumbersome. Writing the book was far less challenging than designing the layout of the manuscript, editing, copyrighting, printing, and promoting it. Luckily my ex-lover-turned-friend, Mally had agreed to represent me as a manager. Though, even with his help, the work was still daunting.

Yet, despite the immense task that lied ahead of me, the work had to be done. I could still hear the Voice of the Creator, "Tell your story!"

And, so, with the urging of the Holy Spirit, I pushed forward.

~~~~

I had been awake late into the night re-editing the manuscript of *I Stood Alone* when it happened; although, I was unaware that it had occurred until an early morning phone call jolted me awake.

"Hello?" Mymomme's usual heavy voice asked into the phone receiver.

"Hello." I responded in my sleep-laden voice.

"Geneva passed away," Mymomme stated somewhat somberly.

"Okay. Thank you for calling me," I replied in my usual detached manner.

Ever since the death of Aunt Carol and my grandfather, Allen, I was no longer surprised when the hand of death visited. Over the past three years, I had lost five family members, all of whom were very near and dear to my heart. No matter how painful their deaths were to me, I had finally come to accept death as a natural part of life.

I stayed in Atlanta during the days leading to Geneva's funeral. I did not attend the fundraiser that Geneva's husband had orchestrated to cover the cost for her home-going services. I did not offer a listening ear or words of comfort to my family members. I did not involve myself in the mayhem of Geneva's funeral arrangements.

I did not want to be near my family. I blamed them for Geneva's demise. For days into weeks before Geneva relinquished her spirit, she had shared with me that she was unhappy in Toledo. She felt unloved and unappreciated by our family. Her husband's acts of infidelity throughout their marriage, including just days before her demise, had finally zapped her of the tenacity to live; her sisters' and brother's mean-spirited ways and selfishness was more than she chose to bear; her child's failure to defend her against the taunts of his wife had drained the life from her. The very people for whom she had once lived had, in effect, killed her.

She looked horrible lying in the casket, clad in a dress that mirrored a remnant of the eighties. Inefficient hands had pumped her frail body with embalming fluids that charred her smooth, golden brown skin to a dark, charcoal-ash color. Her unwashed face revealed traces of adhesive from where a patch covered her chemo-blinded eye.

I sat numb with anger in the church listening to person after person express their sentiments of Geneva. Although, many kind words were shared, few seemed to know the true essence of her spirit. As the last person stood at the podium, I rose to speak.

> *'Chrissie Boo, make sure you speak at my funeral.'* Geneva had asked of me months before her death. Unbeknownst to me, she had planned to die long before she had verbally shared her decision with me.

I informed the nurse of the church that I wanted to say something on behalf of my aunt. The nurse passed the information to Pastor Brooks who replied that I would have to ask the "family" whether it was okay for me to speak. Grief did not allow me to be outraged by the pastor's absurd request; instead, I located my aunt, Cynthia, who conveyed to the pastor that I should be "allowed" to speak.

I stood at the podium for a long moment, scanning the rows of seated attendees before I opened my mouth.

I had a lot to say. I was upset. I was hurt. I felt as though a huge chunk of my soul had been ripped from me. My aunt was gone…my best friend was gone. My eyes began to cloud with tears. I cleared my throat in an attempt to release the tension of unleashed grief that had collected there.

"Geneva was a gentle soul. She represented the true gift of forgiveness. There were many times during the course of our friendship—for she was far more to me than simply an aunt—Geneva would share with me the various misdeeds that had been done against her. I would be livid that anyone could commit such horrible, despicable acts to her. I encouraged her to stand-up for herself and not to suffer their abuse. She would smile as she looked at me and say that she couldn't be strong like me. Her words made me even angrier, because I knew that as long as she allowed people to walk over her, they would. I wanted her to put an end to the viciousness of her assailants."

I browsed the audience, looking into the faces of the attendees. I did not mention anyone by name, though those who had mistreated Geneva knew exactly to whom I was referring.

"And, yet, despite my near-pleas that she take a stand, that she no longer accept the mistreatment of people, she did the opposite: she continued to do kind things to and for them, she continued to love them, and she continued to forgive them…because of this, it is forgiveness for which she is most remembered."

I stepped away from the podium, walked down the long corridor to the front doors of the tabernacle to the great outdoors. I looked at the overcast skies as I shed my blazer, tie, and shirt, until only my undershirt covered my bare chest.

I walked briskly to Mymomme's car. I needed to separate myself from the farce of the home-going service.

I did not want to think of my aunt lying in a casket. I did not want to think of the similarities in her death and those of Mama's. I did not want to remember Mama or Geneva's final words to me.

I tried to force from my mind the thought that Mama and Geneva had died of a broken heart; that disappointment with life and with our loved ones, had hurried the process of death for them.

Opening the car door, I readied myself to make a speedy departure.

"Chris!" I piercing sound of my name rang loudly above the agony of my loss.

With my right leg already in the car, I turned my torso toward the voice.

"Hi!" She waved as she walk-ran to me.

I tried to focus beyond the cloud of tears that had begun to form over my eyes so that I could see the person who called my name; though, it was not until she was nearly upon me, that I recognized her face.

"Oh, hey." I smiled.

"I just wanted to say that I'm sorry for your loss…" the words fell from her tongue gently, soothing my shaken spirit.

"Thank you," I smiled in appreciation.

"I don't want to hold you up. I just wanted to make sure that I spoke before you left."

"Okay. I appreciate you," I smiled genuinely.

Her arms circled my neck as she hugged me long and firmly.

"Call me!" She yelled over her shoulder before she rushed back toward the church.

"Okay, I will!" I yelled back, as I got into the car and started the ignition.

I looked up to see if she was still visible, but she was nowhere in sight. I placed the car into gear and drove from the parking lot as traces of LaNeeka's firm embrace comforted me.

Amid my loss of Geneva, I formally released *I Stood Alone* on the 23rd of October in my hometown of Toledo.

To my great surprise, the book was well-received. I had not expected as many people in Toledo to be interested in reading my story. Yet, my fellow Toledoans pleasantly surprised me with their show of support.

Having gone two years without transportation of my own, I decided to purchase a car. I chose a white, Chevy Camaro. I rationalized the costly purchase of the stylish vehicle by telling myself that it would not only serve my personal needs, but it would also allow me to travel throughout the country selling and promoting *I Stood Alone*. And, that, it did.

After a successful reception in Toledo, I drove to Spring Lake, North Carolina where my cousin, Felicia, arranged for me to have a book signing at her sister's beauty shop. The beautiful, quaint salon was the perfect venue for a small, intimate book reading. A number of Felicia's friends and associates of the community attended the gala, including the future mayor of Spring Lake.

My hopes and dreams for the book were coming to fruition.

~~~

Anger had prevented me from properly mourning the death of Geneva. However, by the time December 17th (Geneva's birthday) had come, my anger had dissipated. In its place, a deep-seated grief consumed me. Sadness and an unquenchable yearning for my friend resided in my spirit.

What would I do? In whom would I turn for guidance? On whose shoulder would I rest my sorrows? In whose loving hands could I trust my tattered heart? Who would listen with a sympathetic ear to my disappointments with life?

Death had robbed me of every special person in my life. Of course, I had many people with whom I loved deeply and who felt the same for me. Though, gone were the persons who most represented the love of God toward me. One by one, they had been plucked from my life. Like petals of a flower on a windy spring's day, each one of them was gone, until I was left all alone in a cruel and uncertain world.

Chapter Six

The last days of the year 2010 had transitioned relatively smoothly, yet the first few weeks of 2011 unveiled unforeseen challenges.

I Stood Alone had received great acclaim, though, in order for the book to reach the masses, I needed to promote it. Initially, Mally and my daddy had agreed to represent me as managers. Mally's knowledge of the entertainment industry was unparalleled to anyone I knew. No matter the genre (singing, dancing, acting, writing), Mally was sure to have an informed opinion of the art. My daddy was attractive, garrulous, and personable—a natural businessman. Together, he and Mally should have been a dream team for any artist; however, they were not.

High tensions boiled beneath the surface of their relationship. They were not disrespectful toward one another, yet a slither of disharmony could be sensed between them, which made working as a team difficult.

Mally was not fond of my daddy as a person. In certain terms, Mally felt that my daddy was a bigot. In truth, Mally's sentiments were well-founded.

Many of my daddy's conversations were laced with prejudicial remarks against gays, women, and Whites. I did not, nor could not have, made excuses for my daddy's behavior.

Over the years, I had become accustomed to his discriminatory vernacular; however, Mally had not grown used to it. As a liberated, gay man, Mally took offense to my daddy's words. He was not disrespectful toward my daddy at all. In fact, he was extremely cordial toward him; yet, he made it known to me that he did not like much of what my daddy expressed regarding women and gay people.

The task of getting Mally and my daddy together for meetings and to agree on small things surrounding the promotion of *I Stood Alone* was far more than I could handle. In the end, I relieved both of them of their responsibilities as my managers; though, without managers, I was unable to move forward with the vision that I had for *I Stood Alone*.

~~~~

Unable to consistently arrange book signings, I began to lag on my car payments. I had purchased a car too prematurely. If I had known better, I would have waited until I had a consistent flow of cash before I made such an expensive purchase. And, if financial matters were not enough, my daddy and I were experiencing yet more discord in our relationship.

"Dad, can I give you some money to pay my car note through your bank account?" I asked as I drove along Highway 78 East through the Georgian mountains late one evening.

"Why do you want to have it paid through my account?"

"Because the financial manager at Wells Fargo asked me if could make the payment through someone else's account…I really don't know. Maybe, the lender would feel more secure if the payment was made through another person's account, since my auto loan is delinquent, but I don't know for certain. He didn't say."

"Let me think about it…Chris, did you tell Sherry not to inform me of your business matters?" My daddy asked abruptly, switching the subject.

Sherry was a friend of my daddy's with whom he had connected me after I relieved Mally and him of their duties as my manager.

"Yea, I did," I responded flatly.

"What's up with that?" He asked.

"Well, you aren't my manager anymore, so I don't want her sharing the personal details of my business with you. I mean, there's no need for you to know them. I know how inquisitive and controlling you can be and, because of your relationship with her, I thought I'd tell her beforehand that I don't want her sharing my business matters.

"Hmmm, yea, okay," he responded curtly.

I could tell by his tone that he was upset, but I did not care. He had the opportunity to help me as my manager. Yet, he had allowed his immature ways and discriminatory feelings against Mally to interfere with his responsibilities as my manager. I would not allow him to micromanage my business dealings through Sherry, as I knew he would have attempted to do so.

"Yea, all right, then," he continued irritatingly. "Well, why would you want your car payment paid through my account, if you don't want me in your business?"

"I said that I don't want you involved in my business matters as it relates to my books. I did not say that I had an issue with you knowing my personal business. The two are not one and the same; though, if you want to mesh them together, you can, and I'll just give the monies to someone else and ask that the funds be drawn from their account," I replied resolutely.

"I don't see why you'd go out and buy a car and you haven't even given me any money for staying at my house," he retorted.

"What??" I asked incredulously. "You said that you didn't want me to give you any money for staying at your house, and that all I had to do was to get me a car!" I exclaimed.

Years prior when I was a teenager, Mama had instructed me to give money to whomever I lived for allowing me to reside the person's residence, even if it was just twenty dollars. Heeding the advice of my grandmother, I offered monies to my daddy for my stay in his home; though, each time that I offered, he ALWAYS adamantly declined the money. Knowing full-well how he was, I should have insisted that he accept the money.

"Yea, well, I didn't know that you were going to get a Camaro."

For some asinine reason, my daddy always had an issue with the cars that I purchased. The first car that I bought after my release from prison was a Grand Am. I did not want the car, particularly because it was previously owned. I did not believe in was in my best interest to buy a used-car. As a poor person, I could not afford to pay for any mechanical failures that may have arisen with a previously owned car, nor did I trust mechanics to be honest and forthright, if the car had a mechanical breakdown. I had known of mechanics that purposely sabotaged cars just to keep a steady flow of monies coming to them.

According to my logic, if I purchased a new car with a factory warranty, any major break-down within the car would be covered by the manufacturer's warranty. I reasoned that my primary obligation in purchasing a new car would be the car note and routine maintenance, as in oil changes and tire rotations.

Yet, despite my better judgment, I listened to my daddy and went to a used-car dealership. I called my daddy on the phone to ask him the specifics in what I should look for in purchasing a used-car. He stated that the car should not be more than two years old; have fewer than 30,000 miles; that a mechanic of my choosing should examine the car; and, that the purchase of the car should include a tune-up and an oil change. With my daddy on the phone with me as I made the purchase, I made certain that all of the specifications that he mentioned were met. Eight months later, the car's transmission malfunctioned. My daddy, who was notorious for always having something to say, was as quiet as a church mouse when I shared with him the dismal news regarding my car.

I had learned from my mistake in buying a pre-owned car. If I did not have to purchase a used-car, I would not.

"So, as long as I get a hooptie, I'm good with you?" I did not wait for him to answer my question regarding buying an old, raggedy vehicle. "Naw, I'm cool. I don't need anybody choosing a car for me, especially when I'm the one who is paying the car note. I'll find somebody else's account to use. Thanks."

"All right, cool," he responded.

I disconnected the call; yet, in my heart, I knew that our phone conversation would not be the end of the ordeal.

Days later, I received a call from my daddy.

"Chris, Sara said to me that the repo people came to the house and that they shined a light in the house, demanding that Sara release your vehicle." My daddy said into the phone receiver.

"Yea, she told me," I replied calmly.

"Well, we don't want your car there. And, she's afraid to be there, so now I have to move back home to be with her," he stated.

Weeks prior, my daddy had moved out of the house that he and Sara shared. Though, apparently, he did not remember telling me a week prior that his current living arrangement was not working in his best interest and that he would have to move back home; so, in truth, his moving back home had very, very little to do with Sara's well-being and more to do with his living situation ending badly.

I chuckled aloud, "Yea, okay."

~~~~

The favor of God was upon me. After my daddy had shared with me that he and Sara did not want my car at their home, my cousin, Janelle, allowed me to live with her in her suburban Atlanta apartment.

I was excited about the move. Janelle was one of my favorite persons. She had a beautiful, gracious spirit, much like her grandmother (my Aunt Carol). Not only did she allow me to live with her, but she also allowed me to sleep in the master bedroom, and she took residence on the sofa in the living room.

In addition to having a place to call home, another one of my cousins, Erica, was in need of an administrative assistant to work at her accounting firm during the busy tax season. Within a few short weeks of working for her, Erica increased my duties to include bookkeeping and accounting duties.

If that was not enough, after just two months, Erica asked me to continue working for her as a full-time employee. With a steady income, I was able to make payments on my car; thereby, avoiding repossession.

~~~~

Uhhh, I DID IT—literally. I did not know how it began…well, actually, I did know how it began, but I did not know why I had allowed it to begin…what I knew for certain—the situation presented itself and I jumped on it—literally, but not in a crass, cocky, kind-of-way.

A relationship that began as a simple acquaintanceship, quickly escalated into much more. She sent me a message on Facebook, expressing that she was interested in purchasing a copy of *I Stood Alone*. I agreed to bring a copy of the book to her home when I next visited Toledo. From that innocent meeting, consistent communication with one another culminated to an invitation for her to visit me in Atlanta. She accepted my invitation and, in April, she drove with her friend to Atlanta to visit for a few days.

She looked like a fish out of water in Atlanta. Her timid, quiet nature seemed foreign in a metropolis filled with boisterous, high-heeled, short-skirt, party-going women. Her casual attire of jeans, a simple top, and mules was uncommon for a visitor to the city.

Most people who visited Atlanta brought with them every designer label they owned—some of which were "knock-off" labels that they prayed would pass for the real thing in their quest to wow onlookers.

During the few short days that she was there, we dined at all of my favorite eateries, had drinks at one of the city's popular margarita bars, and walked the trails of beautiful Piedmont Park.

It was not until the final night of her visit that "it" happened. We lay on our separate sides of a rather comfortable bed in a rather overly-priced hotel room in the suburbs of Atlanta. Beneath the sheets, I could feel the warmth of her skin. I quietly imagined what the softness of her skin would feel like beside and beneath me. I tossed and turned from one side to the other, until an unrelenting curiosity overtook me.

I gently wrapped my arm around her slender waist, slowly pulling her next to me. With her butt nestled against my groin, I softly kissed the back of her neck and shoulders. I rolled her onto her back until I was able to mount her. Face-to-face with one another, the fullness of our lips met as I lifted her bra to expose ample, firm nipples. I sucked them teasingly, flicking each nipple with the tip of my tongue before taking the entire nipple into the warm, juiciness of my mouth. Ambidextrously, I eased my left hand between her legs and slid her panties aside enough for me to locate her vaginal opening. The coarse hairs, coupled with the wetness of her vagina, sent me into overdrive. A moan of ecstasy found its way from my core to my larynx, escaping through my parted lips.

I rolled to my right side, quickly removing my underwear. Moving back between her legs, my tongue kissed and sucked the full length of her outstretched legs. She raised her butt enough for me to remove her panties as my tongue danced between her inner thighs. With great ease, I slowly entered her. Her vagina was tighter than any woman's that I had ever penetrated. Yet, with each thrust, her vaginal walls loosened. We kissed tenderly at first, then with more passion. My momentum quickened. Deeper and deeper, my vagina-deprived member explored every nook and cranny of her treasure chest. I looked at her face. She looked to be in agony.

"Are you okay?" I asked softly.

"Mmmhmm," she mumbled through a pained expression.

"Do you want me to stop?" I asked in concern.

LaNeeka shook her head vehemently from right to left, firmly pulling me back down to her. I resumed my gentle rhythm, then gaining in momentum for several more long minutes, until we were both bathed in my sweat and our passion had reached its climax. Afterward LaNeeka laid on my chest, the rapid pitter-patter of our hearts matching in intensity, until we both drifted into a peaceful sleep.

~~~~

The remainder of the year 2011 went well; that is, until the month of December arrived. I focused my energies on establishing myself in Atlanta. I continued to work at Erica's firm. I moved out of Janelle's apartment and into my own place near Midtown, Atlanta. My quaint, studio apartment was located on the top floor of a newly structured apartment complex. From my balcony, I had a splendid view of Downtown, Atlanta. At night, the glistening glow of the moon and stars looked splendid against the backdrop of indigo-blue skies.

I absolutely loved having a place to call my own; however, my autonomy was short-lived. After only two months in my apartment, Erica announced that she would be reducing my hours at work by half. Initially, I was unperturbed; though, as the realization of what her decision meant, I became livid. Not only would I not earn enough money to cover my living expenses, but Erica's decision to reduce my hours came during the holiday season. I had hoped to be able to afford my niece and nephews a great Christmas, yet that hope had been extinguished.

The following morning, I arrived late to work.

"Hey, Dominique," I greeted my co-worker and friend.

"Hey, Chrissie Boo!" Dominique replied, calling me by my family's pet name for me.

"Hi, Christopher! We didn't think you were coming in today…" Erica greeted from her office, oblivious to the chaos her last minute announcement had caused for me.

"Hi, Erica," I responded as I walked into her office, placing the keys to the office on her desk. "I need to speak with you."

"Okay, Christopher. Have a seat," Erica offered innocently.

"I'm disappointed with the news that you shared with me last night concerning my hours here. I felt like you could have given me some sort of advance notice before you cut my hours. Your actions were callous and insensitive of my circumstances," I said, candidly.

"Well, Christopher," Erica began with the same fixed smile on her face that she had when I entered her office. "You're not given advance notice of a reduction in hours at big corporations…"

"But, Erica, this isn't a big corporation. This is a small firm, and I'm your cousin. I would have thought that, if you didn't have the decency as an employer to make me aware of the decrease in hours, as my cousin you would have let me know what your intentions were, especially during the holiday season."

Erica and I exchanged our feelings about appropriate business etiquettes for several more minutes. Eventually, I realized that we were talking in circles and that, no matter what I expressed, Erica would not understand the position in which I was placed.

While Erica had a gracious, giving spirit, she sometimes failed to consider the needs and feelings of others. I fully understood her position from a business perspective; however, from a humanitarian vantage, her decision seemed selfish and thoughtless.

Without thoroughly thinking through my decision, I resigned from my position at Erica's firm. Though, had I been more mature, I would have kept my job and made the best of my circumstances until the upcoming tax season when business would flourish, again—which was just a few short weeks away. Instead, I behaved like a child who was unaccustomed to the ways of the world.

Chapter Seven

I traveled to Toledo shortly after the New Year. I needed some time away from Atlanta to clear my mind and to decide what my next move would be now that I was unemployed.

From an altruistic point-of-view, it appeared that I had arrived in Toledo not a moment too soon. Everyone's lives were amok: Brandy and LaNeeka seemed to be on the verge of mental break-downs; my brother, Jeremiah, was incarcerated; my nephew, Sharell, was suspended from school; and, Mymomme was suffering from severe loneliness.

During the two weeks that I was in Toledo, I spent as much time as I could with them, giving each of them the time that they seemed to desperately need.

While I was there, I lived with Brandy. The choice to reside with Brandy allowed me to assist her with the care of her son. Jared (Brandy's son) was not a bad child, though he was a teenager. As most parents could have attested, the responsibility of parenting a teenager was cumbersome at times.

Having a male adult in the household was a great help to Brandy as a single mother. Jared listened to the things that Brandy instructed him to do, though usually she had to repeat herself continuously, and to yell while doing so, in order for Jared to do what he was told; whereas, I merely had to ask or mention something to him once and he complied.

~~~~

LaNeeka's spirit was nothing short of glorious. She always went beyond the call of duty to help anyone in need or want. Such an attribute was beautiful and breathtaking to behold, yet, because of her manner of being, LaNeeka found herself being pulled in many directions by many people. While she was efficient at meeting the needs of others, she had not learned how to juggle her varied responsibilities alongside her obligations to herself. My being in town gave her a reason to take a break from fulfilling the needs of others, thereby allowing her to focus on her own needs and wants.

~~~~

Just two months after Geneva's death, Mymomme's partner of over twenty years had succumbed to lung disease. Having lost her sister, both of her parents, and her beau within three years was a difficult burden for Mymomme to bear.

In addition to the passing of her loved ones, Jeremiah, or Miah-Miah as I called him, had recently been jailed for distribution of drugs. Miah-Miah was given a five year prison sentence. While Mymomme and I undoubtedly suffered emotionally as a result of Miah-Miah's incarceration, Sharell, his ten year old son, suffered most from his father's imprisonment, as he was constantly being suspended from school and he had begun to involve himself in illegal activities in the community.

~~~~

I could not believe it! I absolutely could not believe it!

I had only been back in Atlanta for a few days when my world altered once again. The news struck me with the ferocity of a lightning bolt. I did not know her, personally. I had never even met her; yet, those who knew me best, knew that I was an avid supporter of her and the gift with which she had been blessed.

"Awww, Lord! Whitney dead!" My friend, Frank, said to me from across the table as we ate dinner at a popular eatery in Atlanta.

"What?!" I responded to him, not quite believing the truth of his words.

"Whitney died," Frank said as he looked up from his smart phone. "My friend just texted me. I'm reading an article about it online right now."

I sat numbly for a long moment as the weight of Frank's words trickled into my consciousness.

"You okay?" I heard Frank ask from seemingly miles away.

I blinked my eyes, breaking the catatonic stare that held them. "Yea, I'm fine."

I was not fine, I thought, as I chewed the remainder of the dry turkey burger, which I had held in my mouth ever since Frank had delivered the dismal news of Whitney Houston's death.

I wanted to spit the food from my mouth, but I did not want to spoil Frank's appetite. Instead, I laboriously chewed the now flavorless morsels and attempted to swallow around the lump that had formed in my throat. I needed to leave.

"I'm ready to go," I announced suddenly.

"You sure you okay?" Frank asked in concern.

"Yeah, I just need to go home to think," I replied.

"Okay," Frank responded cautiously. "Call me, if you need me."

"I will," I replied as I hugged him before we parted ways.

I walk-ran to my car. Once inside, I quickly turned on the radio. *I Will Always Love You* was being played. I switched stations to FM 107.5. *I Wanna Dance With Somebody*; another of Whitney's songs blared though the speakers. I switched back to FM 104.1 just as the last note of *I Will Always Love You* faded from Whitney's vocal chords.

"Well, folks, if you haven't heard, Whitney Houston is dead at the age of forty-eight. It is a sad day for many of us, as we mourn the passing of a music legend. Whitney was found unconscious in a bathtub at a Beverly Hills hotel…"

I arrived in the parking garage of my home just in time. I quickly placed the gear of the car into park as tears rushed from eyes. I could not believe that Whitney was gone. For most of my teenage years and all of my adulthood, I had loved her. I stood alongside her in the comfort of my home as her voice effortlessly soared and cascaded into a single, piercing note on the stages of the world's largest auditoriums, and I defended her when the world laughed, teased, and ridiculed her because of her drug-addicted antics.

The fierceness of my grief startled me. I usually did not cry easily, especially for someone whom I had never met. Two years prior, when Michael Jackson passed away, I secretly wondered how strangers could mourn the death of someone that they had never known personally. Yet, life had shown me just how an icon's life could be imbedded in the hearts and minds of strangers.

In the confines of my small, white sports car, on the night of February 11, 2012, I sobbed long and hard for the woman whose golden voice had been touched by angels.

~~~

I moved back to Toledo during the last week of February. It seemed that home was where I needed to be. My family needed me there…and, LaNeeka was there.

Ever since the days of my young adulthood when I was caged behind the bars of Lima Correctional Institution, I had dreamed of being in a relationship with a woman. In candor, I had missed the smooth feel of a woman's skin; the soft, wetness of her vagina; the comfort of a woman's presence.

For nearly a decade after my release from prison, I had intentionally chosen not to have relations with women—sexually or romantically—despite my love and appreciation of them.

I did not want to mishandle a woman's heart. I knew that there would always be a part of me that would yearn to be with a man. I did not want to be like countless men—heterosexual and bi-sexual men—who had deceitfully maintained relationships with one woman while having a person(s) of interest on the side. So, I concentrated my sexual and romantic energies into relationships with only men.

By society's standards, I would have been referred to as bisexual; though, for a plethora of reasons, I did not subscribe to the label. I did not like to have my sexual orientation categorized, nor did I like the connotation that was associated with being bisexual.

For some people, the term bisexual indicated confusion or an uncertainty of one's sexuality. Others felt that bisexuals were freaks who simply wanted to have sex with any and everybody. While still others used bisexuality as a means of making the individual feel better about having sex with the same sex (to be bisexual was presumed to be the lesser of two evils).

None of the meanings associated with bisexuality defined who I was as a person. I absolutely did not need anyone or any people to make me feel okay with my sexual/romantic choices. I was very comfortable in who I was. I understood the complexities of my sexual orientation, and I accepted them. As a young teenager, I was fully aware of the parameters of my sexuality. By the time that I had reached the ripe, old age of thirty-eight, nothing had changed—and, from the look of things, it did not seem that they ever would.

Most people viewed things in black and white. Few people conceived of the possibility that a person's sexuality was not always one way or the other; at times, a gray area existed. Rather than to allow people to label me according to the limited constructs of their minds or to give anyone the power to qualify my sexual orientation, I labeled myself in the worst possible way (according to the dominant society) and by a term that the masses clearly understood—gay.

~~~

Despite the knowledge of my sexual orientation and the ramifications of being involved with women, I still longed to be with a woman.

I admitted to myself that I had grown weary of relationships with men. I no longer believed that I would find a satisfying, enduring relationship with a man. I did not have the energy or the desire to contend with the issues that most men presented in a relationship.

Society had so handicapped us men (gay and straight) that we were not able to genuinely share who we were as individuals. Many of us gay men felt that a part of being a man entailed sexually conquering every man whom we met—not unlike the mentalities of ḥeterosexual men with women.

We gay men were so negatively influenced by mainstream society that we attempted to mirror our relationships after those of heterosexuals; in that, there had to be a masculine and a feminine partner: a top (one who penetrates) and a bottom (one who is penetrated).

I had no interest in being a part of the mental gymnastics of the gay mindset. I wanted a love on which I could build; one that would endure the hardships of life; one that would fulfill me emotionally, mentally, spiritually, and physically.

While I did not think that I could find such fulfillment in a man, I believed that I could find it in a woman. LaNeeka appeared to embody every attribute that I wanted in a person. She was loving, kind, family-oriented, and ambitious. Aside from her duties as a nurse's assistant, she was attending school to become a registered nurse.

Proper nutrition and exercise may not have been high on some individuals' list of must-haves in a partner, but they were vital to me. LaNeeka appeared to understand the importance of achieving a harmonious balance in life by attending to the individual selves of the body (mental, emotional, spiritual, and physical).

Exercise was one of the many ways that I had remained of sound mind while I was incarcerated and during the tribulations I experienced after my release from prison. We, humans, encountered far too much mental and emotional anguish in our lifetimes: from the death of loved ones to work-related issues to problems within our families to make-up and break-ups in our romantic relationships. I needed a partner who knew how to balance the demands of life, so that we could more fully embark upon our journey through life together.

~~~

Again, the Creator had shown His favor upon me. Days after moving back to Toledo, a friend of mine offered me a position managing a store of his in suburban Toledo. The store sold smoking products, such as hookahs, smoking pipes, and tobacco paraphernalia.

Although employment at the store was a far cry from working in Erica's firm as an administrative assistant, I appreciated the blessing of a job. I dove into my obligations as manager of the store in the same manner as I did every other responsibility of mine—with care and pride.

The bulk of our clientele at the store consisted of recreational drug users. I held no judgment against any of the customers, many of whom were marijuana smokers from varying socio-economic statuses and races: Whites, Blacks, Latinos, poor, middle-class, and wealthy.

Having experienced my share of hardships, I understood very well the tribulations of living. I treated each and every customer with the respect entitled to every human being. According to my understanding, the decision of how to manage life's woes was theirs to decide, not mine or anyone else's.

~~~

Once again, Brandy had welcomingly allowed me to live with Jared and her in their two-bedroom apartment. I loved staying with them. Brandy had always been far more to me than a cousin, she was one of my best friends; and, Jared reminded me of the son that I never had.

Their apartment was quaint and cozy. Although I slept on the sofa in the living room, I did not mind. In addition to the sofa being incredibly comfortable, I enjoyed the time that we made there as a family: eating, talking, and watching movies together. There was no other person's home in Toledo where I would have wanted to live than with Brandy and Jared.

~~~

While LaNeeka and I had copulated months before my move to Toledo, it was in Toledo that we consummated our relationship by becoming a couple. Sex with her was the first time that I had made love to a woman in nearly twenty years. Our lovemaking was a bit awkward at first, perhaps more so for her than me, as she had only had two partners in her entire sexual history. However, in time, we began to make sparks beneath the sheets, so to express. I relished our lovemaking. I had missed the feeling that a man and a woman shared between themselves while making love.

LaNeeka and I spent huge amounts of time getting to know one another and enjoying one another's company. She regularly came to the store to visit me during her off-hours from school. I looked forward to seeing her smiling face as she entered the store with my favorite snacks (smoothies and chocolate chip cookies). After work, we would go to any one of our favorite eateries, where we would occasionally dine over flavorful margaritas.

Although we thoroughly loved the time that we spent together, it was not long into our courtship that I began to notice peculiarities in her behavior. The events were small, insignificant acts, but nonetheless noteworthy.

"Luda, did you leave the downstairs door open this morning?" Brandy asked me one afternoon.

"Uhn, uhn. Why you ask?" I questioned.

"Jared said that, when he left for school this morning, the door was open," Brandy stated.

"Open or unlocked?" I asked.

"Open," she replied.

"Hmmm, Neeka must have left it open when she left this morning at around six," I said thoughtfully.

"It's not a big deal. I was just curious," Brandy responded, attempting to make light of the situation.

"Well, actually, it is a big deal. I mean, anyone could have walked in here while we were asleep. And, that's not the first time that she's left the door open. The other day she left the upstairs door open…I'm sorry. I'll say something to her about it."

Later that day I expressed my thoughts to LaNeeka concerning the doors being left ajar.

"Neeka, Brandy said that the downstairs door was left open this morning. I think you may have left it open by accident," I stated gently.

LaNeeka's eyes bulged from their sockets. "No-no-no, I didn't! I made sure that I locked the door before I left! I know I did, 'cause I always turn the knob to make sure it's locked! Jared musta did it!"

"Hold on, hold on," I said soothingly. "Calm down. No big catastrophe occurred. None of us was hurt…no intruder entered the apartment. Jared found the door open when he left for school this morning, so he couldn't have done it. And, the other morning, when you rushed out of here, you left the upstairs door open and unlocked. I know for certain that you left it open, because I got up from the sofa to pee right after you left, and Brandy and Jared were still asleep, so they did not leave it open."

"Oh…Oh. Well, I don't know how I did it," LaNeeka replied nervously. "I'll make sure I close and lock them next time."

"It's okay. There's no need for you to be agitated. Mistakes happen."

While I was able to de-escalate the situation, I was still concerned. In itself, leaving a door open or unlocked was not a horrific event. Of course, it was dangerous; though many people had absentmindedly left the doors of their vehicles or homes unlocked without intending to do so. However, the occurrence with the open doors, coupled with other actions of LaNeeka's, gave me pause.

"Neeka, I want to talk to you about something. Initially, I wasn't going to say anything, but I think it needs to be addressed," I said into the receiver of the telephone.

"Okay," she replied quickly; a bit too quickly.

"The other week when we first made love…had sex…I didn't see you for awhile. Why is that?" I asked.

"My mama always told us girls…me…not to pester a guy…to give him his space," LaNeeka replied resolutely.

"Uhm, LaNeeka, I don't think she was talking about…" I paused for a brief moment to find the right words to express my thoughts. "…not in a situation like ours where there is a mutual liking of the other and, more specifically, after you've had sex with the person. I mean, if it's just a wham-bam-thank-you-ma'am then, by all means, do what you will, but, if you like the guy and the guy likes you, and you two are trying to build something with one another, you need to have some sort of communication with him. Again, particularly, if you have had sex with him. I would not let any nigga climb on top of me, penetrate me, and then I don't hear from him, again—again, of course, if it's just a fuck, then you do as you please, but I don't think that's what you were looking for or hoping to have with me." I said, gently; although, I was a bit exasperated.

"Yeah, I see what you mean. I just thought, because of what my mama said, that…uhm…I get what you sayin'," LaNeeka stammered.

"She didn't mean it like that LaNeeka. She meant for you and your sisters not to run around chasing behind a nigga, particularly someone who has no interest in you," I said emphatically.

"Oh, okay. I get it…I get it now," she responded softly.

~~~~

As days slipped into weeks and weeks into months, LaNeeka and I grew closer and closer to one another. We still enjoyed being around each other doing things together. She was a great person through and through. All of the attributes that I sensed were in her when we first met three years prior at Mama's house still applied. She was kind, generous, and loving.

However, in addition to those qualities, I had also come to believe that she was cognitively delayed. How my assumption regarding her mental aptitude had gone unnoticed by me was beyond my understanding. Generally, I was pretty astute in relation to human behavior; though, I did not recognize the indications of a delay in LaNeeka. I had assumed that she was simply quiet and timid and, because of her shyness, she was a bit socially awkward. Though, after spending more time around her, I soon began to realize that more was involved than merely timidity.

"Uh, Neeka, I found this in my food," I said as I entered the kitchen at Brandy's home.

"What is it?" LaNeeka asked, removing the material from my fingers.

"I don't know, but it looks and feels like paper, like the kind on produce."

"Oh, I musta cut up the tomato and put it in the food by accident. I'm sorry," she replied kindly.

"How could you have cut the tomato without seeing the paper or sticker when you rinsed the tomato?" I asked.

"I don't know…I don't know. I guess I wasn't paying attention to what I was doing."

"Okay," I said as I turned to exit the kitchen.

Several more instances occurred in which LaNeeka inadvertently placed things in the food. Initially, I handled her mishaps calmly, but as the many, many acts continued, I began to lose patience with her. I felt like I was Archie Bunker and that LaNeeka was his wife, Edith, of the sitcom "All in the Family." As a child, when I watched re-runs of the show, I used to feel pity for Edith, and I abhorred Archie. However, as an adult in a relationship with a presumed cognitively delayed person, I suddenly understood Archie's frustrations and lack of patience with Edith.

Though, unlike the fictitious character, Archie Bunker, I did not want to be in a relationship whereby I constantly yelled at my partner.

I began to wonder whether I had chosen the right woman with whom to be in a relationship. After thinking of about LaNeeka's wonderful qualities, I began to wonder if the problem rested on me; perhaps, I was simply too impatient. After all, LaNeeka was a great person. I did not know where the issue lay; however, I knew that I would not be with LaNeeka, if I could not control my temper.

"Neeka, I can't do this anymore. I can't be in a relationship with you. This is not how I want to be in a relationship. I don't want to be fussin' and hollerin' at my partner. I did that with those niggas that I was with, but their asses stayed doing stupid shit, like lyin' and cheatin'. You don't do anything and, the things that you do, you can't help. I don't want to yell at anyone, particularly a woman. I respect y'all too much, especially you. You haven't done anything to me to deserve being hollered at. And, you shouldn't accept being hollered at from anybody."

"It don't bother me. My daddy yell at my mom all the time."

"Listen, as much as I love and respect your daddy, I don't want to be like him in that manner. I don't want to be in a relationship whereby I'm professing to love the person, yet I'm constantly hollering at him or her. That ain't healthy. If your father can tolerate your mother's ways, I commend him, but your ways are too much for me. I guess I just don't have enough patience to deal with it. It runs me up the wall that I have to watch everything you do or that I have to double-check behind you like you're a child."

According to LaNeeka, she and her mother had similar minds, or behaviors. In spite of her mother's way, LaNeeka's parents had enjoyed a beautiful, long-loving relationship for over thirty years. I longed to be in a relationship like theirs—minus the yelling.

Although LaNeeka and her mother may have thought nothing of her father's and my yelling, it mattered to me. I was raised by women who consistently yelled at their partners for one reason or another. In my mind, a person yelling was indicative of either unhappiness or a mental disorder. I did not lay claims on either one of them, though, from whichever one I suffered, I did not need to be in a relationship with LaNeeka—or anyone else, for that matter, if I could not control my temper.

"Plus, I'm gay. I don't know what I was thinking about when I decided for us to be intimate. I should have just maintained our friendship," I said, as the full consequence of my action began to weigh on me.

LaNeeka had read my autobiography, *I Stood Alone*, so she knew about my sexual orientation long before we had copulated. We had also discussed my sexual proclivities and romantic relationships with men many times prior to deciding to enter a relationship.

"I don't care that you…or bisexual. We can still be together," she stated, unable or unwilling to apply the word gay to me.

"No, we can't. I don't want to be like my granddaddy, my daddy, my uncles, my cousins, or any number of men who profess to love one woman, but they're playing the field with every woman that they see or, in my case, with every man I see. I'd rather that we be friends," I countered.

"We don't have to be just friends. You can have your guy friends and we can still be together," she offered.

"Uhn uhh. I don't want to do that. I don't want to straddle the fence; I need to stick to one side and stay on it."

"But, you don't have to choose a side," LaNeeka persisted. "I got a lot of gay friends. I know what it's like to be gay."

"What?! That's crazy!" I laughed. "Merely having gay friends doesn't mean that you know what it's like to be gay, and it definitely doesn't mean that you know what it's like to be in a relationship with a gay or bisexual man."

"Uhn-hun, yes, I do. Just do what you want. It won't bother me."

~~~~

Foolishly, I had acquiesced to LaNeeka's suggestion of being with her, while still being intimate with guys as well.

For weeks, we continued harmoniously in our relationship, until I had sex with a guy for the first time since our courtship.

"I can't do this! What if I give you a disease or something?! That would kill me! I don't want to catch anything myself, but it would tear me to pieces if you contracted HIV or something, because of my actions! I just can't do this! I can't be with you, Neeka," I said resolutely.

"You don't have to do it…you don't have to leave me! Don't leave me!" She sobbed loudly from the passenger side of my vehicle.

I knew it would happen. If only I had listened to my inner-intuition. Instead, I allowed my naïve desire to be with a woman to dictate my actions. I should have stayed true to my resolve to be only with men and to deny that part of me that yearned to be with a woman.

I was torn. I genuinely did not know what to do. I knew that I did not want to be in a situation in which I was being untrue to myself. I also knew that I did not want to be in a relationship where my time and energies were divided between two people. I did not want to live two lives. I did not want to fulfill the expectations of ignorant people who would look at me as a pretty boy who preyed on a hapless woman; yet, I did not want to further hurt LaNeeka, either.

And, so, I continued our courtship, of sorts.

Chapter Eight

I should have expected it to happen, especially since I, or we, did nothing to prevent its occurrence. It was not the first time that it had occurred. Earlier in the year, right around the time that the buds of spring had blossomed into summer's glory, it happened as well. Each time that it occurred, I knew long before LaNeeka had clue to what was going on in her body.

"I'm pregnant," LaNeeka expressed solemnly within seconds after she entered my workplace.

"How do you know?" I asked from behind the glass encasement that contained the smoking pipes.

"I went to Planned Parenthood and they told me," she expressed softly.

Despite my insistence that we be only friends, our romantic and sexual relationship continued through the summer and late into the fall.

I had attempted LaNeeka's suggestion of maintaining a romantic relationship with her, while having a relationship with a guy as well, though I could not do it. In addition to the guy and I being incompatible outside of the bedroom, I had always valued monogamy and the sanctity of being in a committed relationship. Having multiple partners simply was not me.

I was constantly in mental and emotional turmoil. A great part of me wanted to satisfy LaNeeka's desire by being her partner; though, a greater need within me urged me to be true to myself.

LaNeeka appeared not to care at all about what I was enduring. It seemed that her chief concern was that I be in her life as her partner. I had begun to resent myself. I had successfully allowed myself to be trapped in a relationship.

Yet, despite the uncertainty of my relationship with LaNeeka, I was ecstatic about the pregnancy.

"Oh, wow!" I exclaimed, as bubbles of excitement began to form in my stomach. "I wonder if it's a boy or girl!"

A smile began to appear across LaNeeka's face. I'm sure she was concerned as to how I would handle the news of her pregnancy. "I think it's too early to tell. The nurse said that I am only a couple of weeks."

"See, I told you that you were pregnant! I could tell! That's the second time and you still an unbeliever!" I laughed triumphantly.

Months before, I had surmised that LaNeeka had conceived a child during the summer. Apparently, while we were copulating, the prophylactic ring that was inserted in LaNeeka's womb had dislodged from its position in her vagina. Because the ring was not in the correct position within her, LaNeeka completely removed the ring from her vagina; though, two days afterwards, she reinserted it into her vagina. Several weeks later, LaNeeka began experiencing excruciating cramps, resulting in her expelling a large glob of blood into the toilet.

According to LaNeeka's doctor, during the two day interim, she had conceived; however, reinserting the ring into her vagina had caused her to spontaneously abort the fetus without ever knowing that she had conceived.

"I didn't know I was pregnant!" LaNeeka laughed.

"Hmmpf, you should have listened to me! I told you that I'm a doctor! I just work at this store 'cause I don't want people knowing all my business!" We both laughed good-naturedly at my joke. "If the baby is a boy, I want him to have my name; if it's a girl, you can name her; although I'd like for Geneva's name to be in the baby's name somewhere, if'n you don't mind," I suggested laughingly.

The excitement of having a baby overshadowed the issues between LaNeeka and me. We focused more on creating a healthy environment in which to raise our baby. However, our dreams for the future of our child were short-lived. Just two days after receiving news of the conception of our baby, we miscarried.

LaNeeka and I were devastated. In just the two days that we had known about our baby, we had already planned his or her future. Our baby's absence left a gaping hole in our lives.

~~~~

Brandy's disposition had begun to irritate. I thought I had grown somewhat accustomed to the ups and downs of her temperament; though, apparently, I had not.

More times than not, when I arrived at her home after work, she had a deep scowl on her face. I could not understand how anyone could go through life unhappy. I had moments of depression and sadness just as anyone else, I presumed, but that was all I had—moments. I refused to wallow in my sorrows.

My list of personal issues were long: I had three degrees, including a master's degree, however, I was working at a tobacco store; I had inexpugnable felony on my criminal record that prevented me from getting work in which I was passionate; I did not have my own home; and, although I was appreciative of having someplace to lay my head, I was thirty-nine years old and sleeping on my cousin's sofa; I had written a pretty decent book, though virtually no one knew of it; I was gay; yet, I was involved in a heterosexual relationship that made me feel as though I was living a complete, bald-headed lie!

Yes, I had plenty of problems, but I refused to feel sorry for myself for more than a good fifteen minutes and not a minute longer! Any time after the allotted fifteen minutes and my mind automatically went into overdrive trying to figure a way to fix the problem.

While I usually did an exemplary job tolerating Brandy's varied mood swings, I could not accept her saying foolish things to me.

"Hey there!" I said enthusiastically to Brandy and her friend, Denise.

"Hey, Chris!" Denise smiled sweetly. "And, don't you come over here givin' me no damn hug and kiss! Don't nobody want none of that shit!" Denise said jokingly mocking her dislike of affection being shown toward her. In truth, she, like many of us, loved to be shown appreciation and love.

"Where you want me to put these?" Brandy said

by way of a greeting. I knew that something was wrong with her the moment she entered the store.

"Oh, I forgot I asked you to bring me those oranges," I said as I made my way around the counter to get the oranges from her.

Brandy and Denise sat on the sofa while we waited for our food to be cooked at the Chinese restaurant next door to the store where I worked. I busied myself by vacuuming the carpet and wiping the glass encasements.

"You vacuum and wipe down that glass every day?!" Denise exclaimed in horror.

I laughed at her outrage. "Yes! That's how David, the owner, wants it done…when in Rome, do as the Romans do!" I replied jokingly, using the Biblical verse to illustrate my point.

For reasons that were unknown to me, Brandy's scowl deepened across her face.

Ignoring Brandy's unpleasant look, "You want to work for me…be my maid?" I joked to Denise, as I repeated a line from the film, "The Color Purple."

Denise was unaware that I was quoting a line from the movie; though in a tone with only Oprah Winfrey could compete, Denise replied, "Hell, naw!"

Denise was as serious as a heart attack! There was no trace of humor or recognition of the movie on her face!

Although Denise did not resemble Oprah Winfrey facially, she was stout and dark-brown in complexion, which did not help the matter! I laughed so long and fully, until I thought that I would lose consciousness!

"I don't know how those people managed to survive slavery. I couldn't have been one of them." Denise stated matter-of-factly; seemingly oblivious to my laughter.

After I was able to control myself a bit better, I replied, "Neither do I! They would have killed me!"

From out of nowhere, Brandy quipped in for the first time since Denise and I had begun talking, "I could see you as a slave; not Denise, but I could you."

I thought Brandy was joking, so I laughed at what I assumed had to be a joke. "How you figure?"

"I don't know…I can just see you as a slave," Brandy replied calmly.

The realization soon dawned on me that Brandy was not joking at all. I looked at her like she was the absolute biggest fool that I had ever seen! Though, rather than to address her foolery, I acted as though she had not said anything.

However, for days afterward, Brandy's comment weighed on my mind. I wanted to have a face-to-face conversation with her about it, though I was unable to do so, because of our conflicting work schedules. Instead, I took a free moment while I was at work to call her at home.

"Bran, I wanted to talk to you about what you said at the store about me being a slave. Do you have an opportunity to talk?"

"Uhn-huh, yea, I do, Luda," Brandy responded.

She was different. Her mood was lighter that day. I had never known for anyone to switch dispositions as easily as her.

"I don't like that you said I would have been a slave," I said, wasting no time and getting right to the reason for my phone call.

"What?" Brandy said innocently. "I did not mean it like that."

"Well, how did you mean it, then?"

"I was just saying that I could see you as a slave."

"Uh, yea, I know. We discussed that part already," I said smartly. "That's what you said before, and that's what I have a problem with," I said irritatingly.

I should have just left the entire comment roll down my back like water does a duck's, but I did not. I could not.

"I was just joking…" She replied innocently. Then, "I mean, what do you do? You not a criminal; you don't break any laws; you probably don't even run a red light!"

"So, are you saying that you were joking or you weren't joking? Because it sounds to me like you meant what you said, especially since you're now following-up what you said with specifics about my behavior."

"I mean, it's not even like that now," Brandy said foolishly referring to the fact that we, African Americans, were no longer slaves.

"Uhh, I know that we are not slaves now. That's not what you were talking about, though…So, are you trying to tell me that, in order for a person to have rejected the system of slavery, they'd have to be a thug or a criminal?

"Well, naw, but…"

I interrupted her. "Do you think that Dr. King or President Obama—two nonthugs—would have accepted the system of slavery?" I did not wait for her to reply before I continued. "Listen, most of my life, I have gone against the status quo, from boldly declaring my sexuality at sixteen years old, regardless of what anyone thought, to enduring seven and half years of incarceration, to moving alone across the country to pursue a dream, to completing three college degrees, to writing a book and working-out damn near every day to maintain my health, in spite of all of the shit that's going on in my life! That is not the mentality of a slave! A subservient slave accepts his circumstances! I don't accept shit! I buck this shit called life every chance I get! If I had a slave's mentality, I would have given in a long time ago!"

"I think you seeing it the wrong way. I wouldn't be offended if somebody said that I could have been a slave."

"Well, let's try it from a different angle: so you tellin' me, if somebody told you that they could imagine you as being a whore in another lifetime, you wouldn't be offend?!"

"No, because I know what I am," Brandy replied.

"Hmpf," I scoffed. "I know damn well who I am, too, but I don't like being paralleled to someone I am not...Maybe you don't take offense to being compared to someone you are not, but I do, especially when the correlation is coming from someone whose opinion matters to me and someone who is as near and dear to my heart as you...Ask your boyfriend how he'd react, if you said that you can see him as being a fag in another lifetime!" I said angrily.

I knew that I should have left the entire situation alone. In retrospect, it seemed silly, but to have someone constantly picking on me based on the whimsicality of her mood was upsetting. Little, minute things quickly became big issues. Every day that I lived with Brandy, I seemed to uncover something new about her. I had always known that she was moody and, at times, mean; however, what I did not like is that she behaved bully-ish toward me. She was used to the kind-Chris whom adored her and who treated her with the upmost respect. Sadly, her behavior was reminiscent of many other people's; in that, oftentimes a person had to show a less than pleasant side of himself to be treated with the dignity entitled to every person.

Unfortunately, she would learn the hard way, I surmised.

~~~

I was not clairvoyant, but I knew it would happen. I knew me and I knew her. She could not help herself and, although I had tried to control myself on many occasions, I could not help myself, either. It was just a matter of time.

Everything happened so quickly that the exact reasons for the conflict were unknown to me. I recalled Mymomme sitting on the sofa as I prepared to dress for the day. I remembered trying to explain something, and, then, it happened.

"I'm taaaaaaalkinggggggggg!!!" Brandy yelled from the top of the stairwell leading to her bedroom.

I lost any sense of composure that I had, matching and exceeding the volume of her voice, I roared, "I don't give a fuck if you are talking! I don't know who in the hell you think you are! Yelling at me like I'm a motha fuckin' kid! I ain't none of yo damn son! You talk to Jared's ass that way, but you ain't gone talk to me any kind of motha fuckin' way!" I sneered.

I was incensed. I had lost every bit of control over my emotions. I was beyond livid. I angrily began snatching my clothes from the sofa, so that I could quickly dress and get out of her apartment, when suddenly the world around me began to soften. My eyes suddenly took in the figure of the person sitting on the sofa. *Oh, my God!* In my rage, I had become oblivious to her presence.

"I'm sorry," I muttered sincerely to Mymomme. I did not believe in cursing around my parents or elders, no matter my age.

"It's okay," she said as a faint smile appeared on her face.

The slight trace of pride on her face caught me off guard. I did not wholly know the reason for Mymomme's satisfaction. Two possible conclusions that I surmised were: she had witnessed me accept Brandy's cantankerous nature too many times and that she was pleased that I rebuked her behavior; or, she was jealous of the immense love I had for Brandy and she took pleasure in our discord.

~~~

I was leaving—again.

Terry, my employer and good friend, had announced that he was closing the store where I worked. Business had not done as well as he had hoped, so he chose to relocate the store to Akron, Ohio.

Although I would miss being gainfully employed, I was delighted to leave Toledo. I could not tolerate another winter in Ohio. I did not care what anyone said about me being raised there or how accustomed I should have been to the snow, the ice, or the cold! I did not like any of those elements! Let the Eskimos and whomever else that wanted to live in such conditions endure them, but not me!

Plus, Brandy had truly gotten on my ever-last nerve—for real. The woman had gone and got a dog! I had nothing against animals. In fact, as a spiritual being, I felt that animals were entitled to love and respect, just as humans. However, I was not raised around animals; that is, although we had dogs, they were outside-dogs, meaning they lived OUTSIDE. My grandfather, Allen, had built a 12x12 cage and a doghouse inside of the cage for them to live OUTSIDE. They never came into the house—ever! Allen, my cousins, and I would let the dogs out of the cage to run around the yard, but they did not enter Mama's house.

Brandy was a different kind of Black person than I had ever known. She did all kinds of stuff with that dog: she cuddled him, checked inside his mouth, examined his rectum—and, all with her bare hands! I was well-aware that some new-aged Black folk treated their dogs like members of the family, but I had never encountered a member of my family treating a dog in such a manner. I had only seen people on television do the things that she did with that dog, and those things that I saw on television were done by White people, never, ever a Black person!

I sincerely did not have an issue with what Brandy did with the dog, per se. It was her prerogative if she wanted to be her dog's personal veterinarian. The thing that sent me over the edge was when she consistently invited the dog to lie on the sofa with her when on many occasions I instructed him not to get on the sofa. Again, I could have cared absolutely less what she did with the dog, as far as being his personal dentist and veterinarian, but her sofa served dual purposes: a place on which for us to lounge while watching television AND as my bed. I understood full-well that it was her apartment and her sofa to with whatever she pleased, but I could not lay my head where a dog had his paws, butt, underbelly, or genitalia, regardless of the fact that I placed a sheet over the sofa before I went to sleep. The entire act of the dog being on the sofa where I sat, slept, and sometimes ate was vomit-inducing to me. Brandy's repeated invitation to the dog for him to parley on the sofa, especially after I had told him not to lounge on it, was a clear indication that it was time for me to get out of there—and, fast!

~~~~

My brother, Corey, and I had moved to Atlanta together. We arrived at Mother Dear's (our stepmother) house during the wee hours of the morning. Dad and Mother Dear had separated months before our arrival in Atlanta. As such, we had free-rein to the living quarters in the furnished basement.

Corey and I were excited about our move to Atlanta. Of course, I had lived in the southern metropolis before; though, for Corey, it was his first time living there. It was also the first time that we had lived in a city together as adults. We excitedly made plans of going to clubs and house-parties together.

A decade before, at the age of eighteen, Corey admitted to those closest to him that he was gay. The information came as no surprise to me. I knew he was gay, or soon would be, when I first laid my eyes on him after my release from prison twelve years prior. He was only a child of sixteen at that time, though I still could sense that he was gay.

The truth of my assumption was evident in his behavior and his social circle: his closest friends were primarily females, two of whom included our female cousins; he loved clothes more than most women I knew; and, he was not exactly effeminate, but he was not entirely masculine either—in short, he reminded me of a younger version of myself.

Before we settled into our new home environment, I told Corey that we should pay Mother Dear rent for staying with her. I informed him of what Mama had instructed me years ago regarding staying with someone, even family members. I also shared with him the situation that I had with Dad concerning living in his home and paying rent. I let Corey know that, even though Dad had insisted that I not pay him for living in his home, he later rescinded on what he said.

"Although Dad and Mother Dear are no longer together, he still tries to exercise his control over her and her household. Give her what you can and you'll be grateful in the long run."

Past experiences had proven to me that it was better to be safe than sorry.

~~~

I did not always exercise good sense. Even when I knew better, I still made goofy and, seemingly, thoughtless decisions. My relationship with him was no exception.

Our initial meeting occurred on a gay chat site. For weeks we had chatted through the social app before we exchanged telephone numbers. Several more weeks passed before we actually met face-to-face at a McDonald's near Mother Dear's home. Eventually, after a month or so of our first in-person meeting, I invited him to visit me at Mother Dear's house.

His name was Troy. He was attractive: thick built, skin the color of a dark, ripened plum, and jet-black, wavy hair that glistened radiantly. He was intelligent, charming, and goal-driven. Yet, despite all of his attributes, I immediately knew he was not the guy for me. He was all the things I liked in a person, but he was not the one. Perhaps, it was his age, as he was only twenty-six years old. I was not certain; though, there was something about him that just did not gel well with me romantically.

After several conversations with Troy, he shared with me that he had a bachelor's degree in business. As he continued to talk, he went on to explain to me the parameters of his education and his professional experience.

"Maybe you can represent me as a manager...I am not business-minded at all!"

"I'd love to!" Troy exclaimed.

Although Troy did not have any experience as a manager and, more specifically, as a manager to an author, he was personable, out-going, and he was determined to represent me well.

Troy sold a few books just within the first couple of weeks of representing me. He also arranged both short and long term goals: poetry readings in the Atlanta area to familiarize people with my work and me; and, book signings at national conventions during the summer. We also agreed that I should retain a public relations manager to arrange radio and television appearances.

In time, Troy and I settled into a comfortable business relationship. Yet, despite all that I heard about mixing business with pleasure, I went against the experiences of others and began to date Troy.

~~~~

While Corey and I were living with Mother Dear, the three of us had settled on a fair amount to pay Mother Dear each month for living in her home. Although the amount was attainable for me, gathering the funds was sometimes burdensome for Corey who was unemployed at the time.

Despite Corey being without work, Mother Dear still expected him to pay her rent. I did not take issue with Mother Dear expecting him to pay rent—necessarily. As an adult man of twenty-eight years of age, if Corey lived someplace else, he would have still been expected to pay rent. However, I was bothered by the fact that Corey was expected to pay rent, but our sisters, Tiana and Tatiyana, were not made to pay for their lodging in Mother Dear's home.

"Hey, Mother Dear. Do you have a moment to talk?" I asked as I entered the living room where Mother Dear sat grading her students' homework, as she was a middle school science teacher.

"Mmhmm, yes, I do," she responded, placing her work aside.

"Corey told me that you asked him for his portion of this month's rent. I understand that Corey is grown, but I don't think it is fair that you expect him to pay rent, but not our sisters who are technically adults as well, being that they are eighteen and twenty-four."

"Well, Tatiyana doesn't have a job and Tiana is waitressing and doesn't really have much money," she offered.

"Yes, but Corey isn't working at all; yet, you still expect him to pay rent. I'm fine with the amount that we agreed upon; I can afford it. In fact, I wouldn't have it any other way; I would not live here if I couldn't pay you something every month for my stay. I am almost forty years old. I need to pay for my stay wherever I live."

"Well, you're the one who suggested that you all pay rent here," Mother Dear countered.

"Yes. That's, because, as I said, I am grown. I do not nor can I expect to live somewhere rent-free. I also remember my experience with Dad the last time that I lived here. I was not going to place myself in a position to endure anyone throwing in my face that I did not pay rent for my lodging. As it relates to Corey, you and I both know how Dad feels about Corey. Although you two are separated, I know that he still has some influence into your personal matters.

I did not want your relationship with Corey to be tainted by the way that Dad feels about him or the way he treats him."

"Oh, no! I wouldn't do that; I wouldn't let Andrew control me like that."

"Well, Mother Dear," I said gently. "You have already allowed Dad to have some influence or control of you. For instance, your view of Corey as lazy and self-serving, which may be true, largely comes from what Dad says about Corey. I know that Corey isn't quick to cut the grass and that he does the bare minimum around here, by way of cleaning, but your perception of him was initiated by Dad, and you know how Dad is toward everybody. I don't mean to make you feel bad, but you've never treated Corey and me the way that you treat Tatiyana and Tiana. I know that you are our stepmother and that you're their biological mother, but you've known me for thirty-four years, since I was five years old. I love you like I love Mymomme and my daddy. I don't make a difference between you and them. And, although Corey was conceived during your relationship with Dad, he shouldn't be held accountable for what his mother and Dad did," I said sensitively.

"No, I wouldn't treat him or you two differently than I do my girls," Mother Dear replied contemplatively.

"But, you already do; and, expecting him to pay rent and not expecting the girls to pay rent is just one example of the difference that you make between us and them. I will give you the money that he owes you, though," I said as I stood to get the money to give to her.

I returned a couple of minutes later with Corey's portion of the rent. Mother Dear looked preoccupied with her thoughts. I gave her the money, hugging her before I left her to digest what we had discussed.

~~~

Initially, everything seemed to be going well between Troy and I. I still was not comfortable with the choice that I had made to date him, but his positive qualities seemed to override my trepidation. At first, we were able to keep separate our two relationships. However, within a few months of beginning our business relationship, things had changed.

"What do you mean you didn't want to sell a calendar to him?" I asked of Troy irritatingly.

"I'on want him looking at your body like that," Troy responded in his Georgian accent.

"What?! Are you crazy?! This is business! This is about getting me and my work out there, so that people know who I am, not about you not wanting your friend to see my body! I thought you said that you could separate our relationships?" I asked bewilderingly.

"You're right...I just don't want him to see you like that...I can keep the relationships separate. It won't happen, again."

"Evidently, you can't keep them separate!" I replied angrily.

In time, I moved pass Troy's possessiveness toward me. We continued with both of our relationships; though, soon, another situation arose.

"Troy, did a guy come by the booth expressing an interest in my work?" I asked.

At Troy's suggestion, I rented a booth at a book expo in Atlanta. The event was to be attended by hundreds of people.

"I was told that a guy, whom introduced himself as a director, came to our booth, made a remark about how attractive he thought I was, inquired as to my whereabouts, and then gave you his business card to give to me. Did this occur?"

"Yea, I think so..." Troy responded noncommittally.

"Huh? Do you realize that he could have possibly directed the screenplay that I just wrote to *I Stood Alone*?"

"Yea, well, you know how I get. I don't like these dudes liking you."

Ughhh! If good sense did not tell me before, I surely realized at that moment that I should not have ever entertained both relationships with Troy. The problem was: I was several days late and quite a few dollars short of the realization.

"Uh, Troy, we discussed this. You said that you could handle this; that you could separate your personal feelings from our working relationship."

"I thought I could."

"Listen, I appreciate what you've done for me; I really do, but we're going to have sever our relationship."

And, just like that, I was yet again without a manager. The whole business of promoting my work was proving to be too much for me. I was perplexed as to what step to take next. I had done what the Creator had instructed of me by writing the book. I did all that I could to share my story with the world; though, to no avail. I was tired of struggling; tired of living with family members; tired of living in poverty.

It was time that I earned a better living for myself; it was time for me to relinquish my vision for *I Stood Alone*.

Chapter Nine

My life was in shambles. I could not get a job, because of the nineteen year-old felony on my record; my book was not selling; and, I was penniless.

I did not know in what direction to go, so I moved northward—back to Toledo. However, another problem presented itself in moving home: I had nowhere to live. I did not want to live with Brandy, again; I did not want to move into Mother's house, as my cousin, Casha, was living there; and, living with Mymomme was not even a thought worth considering, as she lived in a one-bedroom apartment. Experience had taught me that not everyone is meant to live together, no matter the relationship or the love that the two may share for one another.

"I got a idea," LaNeeka expressed to me on a late summer's day. "How about I get a apartment and you can live there with me?"

"Huh?" I asked quizzically.

"I can get a apartment, and we can stay together. I need to move out of my parent's house, anyway. They gettin' on my nerves," she suggested eagerly.

LaNeeka and I had remained in constant contact after my move to Atlanta in February.

After the miscarriage of our baby a few months prior, our romantic relationship soon fizzled. Yet, in spite of my move to Georgia, nothing had really changed in our dealings with one another. We still talked on the phone every day, and we still visited one another regularly.

"I don't know. That seems too much like marriage!" I laughed, partly joking; the other part completely serious.

"No, it won't," she replied, missing the humor in my statement. "We can have separate bedrooms. I won't bother you."

"Hmmm, I appreciate the offer, but I need to think about it," I said.

As much as I wanted to say no to LaNeeka's offer, I did not know of any other person with whom I would feel comfortable sharing a space, since I did not want to stay with Brandy. Once again, life would show me that sometimes it is best to leave well-enough alone.

~~~

Several weeks later, LaNeeka and I moved into "our" apartment. Still unsure of what direction in which to go in my life, I enrolled in school at Bowling Green, where I had achieved a bachelor's degree. I surmised that I could take a few classes toward a doctorate in psychology to pass the time while I was deciding what to do with my life. I could not imagine being in Toledo, or anywhere else for that matter, without doing something productive.

The school year began well. I enrolled in two psychology courses. By the middle of the semester, I had maintained a high "B" average in both courses. I was not satisfied with the "B's", though I figured I had several more weeks of class to raise the grades to A's. However, before such an endeavor could take form, I received disheartening news from my physician.

It was a blast from the past. Years prior, my general practitioner told me that he believed I had cancer. As fate would have it, I did not have cancer. The physician erroneously assumed that I had cancer because of elevated levels of a specific protein in my blood.

The second time was no different; except, in the more recent instance, I was actually exemplifying some of the symptoms of cancer.

After having my yearly physical performed, my general doctor called me into the office to discuss my test results.

"Christopher, your PSA results have come back. Your number is above fifty. A healthy number is between one and eight," the Indian physician expressed gravely. "PSA (prostate specific antigen) registered abnormalities in the prostate. Generally, when a patient has a number that is as so high, he is positive for prostate cancer. I am referring you to an oncologist. Be certain not to miss your appointment, Christopher."

I was stunned. As a forty year old, African American, I had a higher risk of developing prostate cancer than males of other races. In addition to the abnormal PSA reading, I had begun to have trouble urinating; dribbles of urine flowed from my penis at an agonizingly slow rate; and no semen discharged when I ejaculated.

As with the time before when I was given a premature diagnosis of cancer, I believed the physician's report. And, like the time prior, I had begun to mentally plan for my demise. I thoroughly researched the symptoms of prostate cancer and its treatment. Based upon my symptoms and the factors of my age and race, there was a very likely chance that I had the disease. I had already settled in my mind that I would not endure the torture of chemotherapy or surgery.

Yet, as fate would have it, in the end, it was determined that I did not have prostate cancer. Instead, I had acquired a bacterial infection of the prostate, for which I was treated with antibiotics. After a month of taking the high-dosed medication, my PSA had been reduced to a healthy number of seven and the infection was gone.

~~~~

LaNeeka and I decided to celebrate Thanksgiving at the apartment we shared. I awakened during the early morning hours to prepare a dinner of baked and oven-fried chicken, macaroni and cheese, dressing, and several homemade cakes; LaNeeka added to the feast by cooking a huge pot of collard greens, fresh rolls, and potato salad. We stuffed over fifty family members into the small, two-bedroom apartment. Every corner of the rooms in the apartment was filled with family from new-born infants to old-aged adults, though everyone left with satisfied bellies and gracious spirits.

Several days after thanksgiving, I announced to LaNeeka that I was riding with my daddy to Atlanta to begin writing my next autiobiography. I needed some time away from the dreary coldness of Toledo. During the tense period of believing that I had cancer,

I had withdrawn from my psychology classes at Bowling Green, so I had ample time with which to write.

~~~~

I was gone for three weeks. It was the longest time that LaNeeka and I had ever been away from one another since we had begun living together. Perhaps, writing the manuscript for my book had allowed me to be more in tuned with my feelings or, maybe, it was the mere fact that LaNeeka was a beautiful person. Whatever the source of my feelings, I had begun to falter in my resolve to only be friends with LaNeeka.

The knowledge that I loved LaNeeka was no surprise to me; nor was I shocked by the depth of my love for her. LaNeeka was an exceptional person: her spirit was comparable to none; her devotion to work as a caretaker was outstanding; her love of me was unparalleled. She loved me sweetly and innocently, purely and majestically. The favor of her love was a gift from the Creator to me; a wondrous synthesis of the great loves of my life: Mama, Mother, and Geneva.

Our love of one another beckoned me to her. At first sight, we embraced each other with a savage fierceness; a longing of not only one another's presence, but also of our spirits and of our genitalia...

~~~

My old friend, John, for whom I worked at the tobacco store, offered me another managerial position at his store in Akron. Although Akron was two hours east of Toledo, I welcomed the opportunity to earn an income without hesitation.

LaNeeka's phone call came just as the sun had begun to fade from the sky. I answered the call somewhat irritatingly, as she and I had not parted on good terms.

"Hello?" I said into the phone receiver.

"Hi, Chris. I just wanted to tell you...I went to Planned Parenthood...I, I'm, uhm, I'm pregnant." LaNeeka stammered.

My stomach somersaulted within my abdomen. Pregnancy was not the information that I had expected to receive.

"How far along did the doctor say you are?" I asked calmly.

"Uhm, she, uhm, the nurse said that I'm approximately six weeks."

Hmmm. I knew that my feeling was correct. I could pinpoint the exact moment that LaNeeka conceived. As always, I knew she was pregnant; not only did LaNeeka look physically different to me, but I also felt the difference in myself. It was as though I was sharing my spiritual space with someone. Obviously, a physical portion of me had been created, but I felt that a part of the essence of who I was had left my body and entered into the universe.

"Okay. We need to decide what we're going to do," I said.

"Yea, I know," LaNeeka said softly.

For as long as my young teenage years, I had wanted to be a father. In part, my desire arose from the need to love someone. I wanted someone in whom I could call my own. Because my own young life had been littered with so much pain and feelings of being unwanted, I wanted to pour the great love that I had caged within me into a child of my own. I longed to give another being what my parents had not given me—wholesome love, security, and a sense of belongingness.

While the whimsical wants of my youth were still present in me, as a forty-year-old man, they were tempered with reality. I was in no position to fulfill the needs of a child. Although I was loving, kind, giving, and understanding, I wholly understood that those attributes did not meet all of the needs of what it entailed to be a parent.

"I'll be home tonight," I said.

~~~

Over the course of the next few weeks, I vacillated between accepting the gift of life with which God had blessed LaNeeka and me and with the obvious truth of my circumstances: I could not fulfill the needs of a child.

Although I felt blessed that John thought of me as often as he did, I could not raise a child with an uncertain job that paid a little more than minimum wage. Despite having achieved three college degrees and having written an engaging book, the reality of my situation rested on my criminal record, which largely prevented me from being gainfully employed. I could not imagine knowingly bringing a child into the world with the knowledge that I could not provide for him or her in the manner that I would have liked.

My relationship with LaNeeka was also a major factor worth considering. Technically, we were not in a romantic relationship. Although LaNeeka was a remarkable person, and I loved and valued her with every fiber of my being, I could not deal with her cognitive delay. As a whole, she was an incredibly mature and capable woman; though at times, I felt like I was involved in a relationship with a teenager, rather than a grown woman.

My parents were yet another factor as to the cause of my mental acrobatics. I loved my parents profoundly; though, in truth, they were not always kind individuals. All things considering, I had weathered my parents' ill-ways well; however, I did not know how I would behave if they treated my child in the same manner that they had treated most everyone else in their lives, including my siblings and me.

~~~

The scene had occurred many times before; the variables were the only difference. The first time it happened several years prior. I had just moved back to Toledo from Atlanta and LaNeeka and I had just finished making love. After I had reached my climax, I went to the bathroom to wash myself. While in the bathroom, I smelled a rancid odor emitting from the area surrounding my penis. I stood in the bathroom for several more seconds trying to decide how I would share the information with LaNeeka. Finding no way of expressing my thoughts, other than with the truth, I re-entered the living room.

"Neeka, smell my penis," I stated matter-of-factly as I entered the room.

LaNeeka looked at me quizzically as she folded the towel on which we had lain.

"It's cool," I laughed. "I just want you to smell something."

Hesitantly, LaNeeka leaned forward to smell my genital. She sniffed and then sat back in her seat.

"You smell that?" I asked.

"Uhn uh, no. What I'm supposed to smell?" LaNeeka asked sincerely.

"You don't smell that?" I asked astonishingly.

"Uhn uh."

"There's an odor. I think it may be coming from you," I said gently.

"Uhn uh, that ain't coming from me. Uhn uh...Uhn uh," she said agitatedly, with her eyes nearly bulging from their sockets.

"I thought you said you didn't smell anything?"

"Uhn uh, that ain't coming from me...that ain't coming from me."

Her behavior was beyond bizarre to me. I well-understood how it must have felt to have your lover telling you that a foul odor may be coming from your vagina, but her agitation did not seem normal to me, even under the circumstances.

"Neeka, I wouldn't lie to you...I smelled an odor before, when we first had sex in Atlanta, but I didn't know how to say it without hurting your feelings."

For a moment, LaNeeka seemed to consider what I said; then, "Uhn uh, that ain't coming from me."

"Neeka, it's cool. It's not uncommon for a woman to have a vaginal odor every now and again. Just get some vaginal wash or douche; it should help with the odor."

"Uhn uh, my mama said only hoes use vaginal wash!" She stated emphatically.

"Huh? That's not true! Lots of women use vaginal wash: Mymomme, Mama, my aunts! I used to see their douche bags under the bathroom sink when I was a kid, and they used Summer's Eve and Vagisil, too! Not all women who use that stuff are whores or prostitutes!" I said adamantly.

On a deeper level, LaNeeka appeared to be accepting the truthfulness of my words, yet outwardly she still resisted.

"I, I, I'll go to see my doctor, but I know that ain't coming from me!" LaNeeka stammered persistently.

Another instance occurred nearly two years later as we lay in the bed.

"Neeka," I began softly. "I think you're going to have to shower before we make love…"

"Okay," she replied.

I waited for LaNeeka to ask me why, when there was no query, I stated my reason for offering the suggestion.

"I smelled stool when we made love the other day."

"Hmmm?" She asked.

"When we were making love the other day, I smelled stool."

"Oh! Hahaha," she laughed. "That's from me passing gas! Hahaha, my daddy just said me and my sisters got some strong ass gas! Hahaha!"

"Neeka, this is not gas," I said calmly, although I was becoming angry.

"Hahaha, yes, it is! I'm tellin' you, my gas is strong!"

"Listen, Neeka, I wasn't born yesterday! I know the difference between the smell of gas and shit! And, this was shit!"

"Uhn uh, my da…"

"...Listen, I don't care what your daddy said! I love and respect the man, but this is not no damn gas! And, you need to quit saying that silly shit! It is not a big deal, but you are making it one! All you have to do is wash your ass, if you know we are about to have sex, or use those disposable wipes that I have in there to wipe my ass after I shit!" I said angrily.

"Okay, but I'm telling you, my gas..."

I thought it was rude to interrupt anyone when they were talking, but when I was upset and when I felt like I was being bombarded with senseless statements, I could not control myself.

"Listen, girl, don't nobody's damn gas stick to their ass like that, unless the gas is laced with shit! Quit trying to tell me that it's gas! Gas dissipates in the air! It doesn't cling onto your damn skin all damn day! I can't believe we're having this conversation about something that's fixable! I understand that it may be embarrassing for me to tell you about an odor that's coming from you! I get that, but if I can't tell you, then who can?!

That boy, Michael, that I was in a relationship with in prison, once told me that my breath had an odor! Do you think I went crazy, denying it, and making-up all sort of excuses as to its origin?! No, I brushed my teeth more often, I brushed my tongue every time that I brushed me teeth, and I used mouthwash, but I didn't do all this bullshit you doin'!" I said exasperatingly.

I truly could understand how LaNeeka may have felt uncomfortable with me sharing such intimate information with her; however, her reaction was the same, no matter the topic of discussion. I used to jokingly tell her that, if I said that there was a piece of lint in her hair, her response would be the same: 'Uhn uh, no, no, no, ain't no lint in my hair!'

~~~

My mind was everywhere: at times, I felt that I could make a romantic relationship with LaNeeka work, despite being gay; at other times, I felt that there was no hope and that nothing I did would ever create a healthy, functional relationship with LaNeeka.

Although I was flabbergasted with LaNeeka's inability to accept constructive criticism, her actions were not the straw that broke the camel's back. Such a dishonor belonged to me.

Late one evening, as I prepared to eat, I had forgotten to get a fork from the kitchen with which to eat my food.

"Neeka, can you bring me a fork, please? I forgot to get one," I asked from the living room.

"Yes," LaNeeka said from the kitchen.

Seconds later, LaNeeka brought a fork to me.

"Okay. Thank you," I said as I received the fork from her hand. Just as I was about to put the fork in my food, I saw that it was not clean. "This fork is dirty," I frowned as I stood to walk into the kitchen to get another fork.

"I rinsed it off," LaNeeka said in her defense.

"You couldn't have rinsed it off, because it's dry," I replied.

"Yes, I did! I dried it off before I gave it to you!"

"Well, if you rinsed and dried it, why didn't you see that it was dirty? Never mind," I stated tiresomely.

"I'm telling you I did! I remember rinsing it and wiping it off! I'm telling you!" She said insistently.

"Okay. Whatever. It's cool," I pulled open the drawer containing the silverware. It was empty. I opened the dishwasher to get one that had recently been washed, though not yet put away in the cupboard. Every piece of silverware that we had was lodged into the small compartments that held the silverware. I retrieved a fork from one of the sections, it was dirty; I grabbed another one; it, too, was dirty.

"These are all dirty. Neeka, you can't put all of this silverware in here like this. They're not getting clean. The water and detergent can't even get to them, because they are so tightly packed in here," I said as I began putting the soiled silverware in the sink to be hand-washed.

I was tired and frustrated. Again, I felt the overwhelming sensation of being in a relationship with a teenager, instead of a thirty-five-year-old woman. She partially-did everything! I had to explain seemingly everything, as though I was instructing a child. *Not everything should have to be explained; some things should be a matter of common sense*—the thought resonated over and over in my mind.

I began to wash the silverware that I had tossed into the dish water in the sink. I turned on the water to rinse the silverware before I placed them in the dish rack; however, without saying excuse me, I forcefully reached pass LaNeeka, bumping her with my forearm. LaNeeka stumbled to the side from the force of my action.

I dropped the silverware into the sink, "I can't do this…I'm not going to do this. This relationship is unhealthy enough with everything else that is going on between us and, now, I'm putting my hands on you! I can't do this! I'm out!"

I was absolutely finished with whatever semblance of a relationship that LaNeeka and I shared together. I hurriedly walked from the kitchen and into the bedroom where I packed my clothes. To have expressed that I was hurt and ashamed of myself would have been the greatest understatement of the century. Throughout all of my childhood, I had seen Mymomme's lovers fight her; I had seen Allen, my grandfather, stab Mymomme in the leg with a brass ashtray as he beat her; I watched Allen and Mama fight; I saw Allen punch a hole in a wall, in an attempt to punch Geneva in her face; I had seen Aunt Rachel and her father's children fight; I watched my Aunt Kim's husband violently drive his car onto the front porch of Mama's house in retaliation against Aunt Kim.

My entire childhood had been filled with violence; though, more specifically, it had been filled with violence against women. As a child, I had vowed that I would never place my hands on a woman in anger for as long as I lived! And, yet, there I was as an adult man bumping, pushing, or whatever my action was a woman who I professed to not only love, but who was also carrying my unborn child.

I cried uncontrollably as I placed my clothes in my luggage. I could not erase the collage of images of the women in my family being assaulted by men. I was thoroughly disgusted with myself for allowing myself to touch LaNeeka in any way that was not laced with love; though, equally as disappointed with myself for remaining in a relationship that I had allowed to change me into someone that I was not.

~~~

With my luggage in tow, I arrived at Mymomme's apartment during the early morning hours.

"What's wrong? You and LaNeeka not getting along?" Mymomme asked moments after she opened the door to let me into her apartment.

I hesitated before answering. I had learned long ago not to share personal information with Mymomme. Yet, against my prior experiences with her, I shared my thoughts and feelings. "No, I can't do it anymore…I can't be with her. I'm going to ask her to have an abortion."

"Boy, let that girl have that baby!"

"Uhn uh, I don't want to raise a baby under our circumstances: I don't have a job; we're not getting along; and, I pushed her or bumped her."

"That don't mean nothing. Y'all can still have that baby."

I had not really expected Mymomme to understand my sentiments. Abusively dysfunctional relationships were commonplace to her: she had endured, her mother had endured them, and her sisters had endured them. In a strange, unhealthy way, physical, mental, and verbal abuse were normal to her in a romantic relationship.

"No, I don't want a baby of mine being raised in an unhealthy environment," I said.

"It'll be all right. Look at you, you turned out all right."

"Yeah, that's by the grace of God. I don't want my child to endure what I did, not to say that he or she will, but I don't want it to potentially suffer needlessly. I don't have a job or any means of supporting a baby, and now I'm being physically abusive toward LaNeeka. I can't do it."

"Boy, y'all can stay together. Ain't nothing wrong with her," Mymomme said in LaNeeka's defense; although, I had not said anything about her.

"I'm not saying that anything is wrong with LaNeeka. I'm saying something is wrong with me. I can't deal with her ways, as kind and loving as she is, I don't have the patience. And, I don't want my child being raised like that; in a verbally, or now, physically abusive environment."

"Don't make that girl have no abortion," Mymomme said as she closed the door to leave for work.

Mymomme simply did not understand the issues that were involved. We, African Americans, were given a very, very minute` window of opportunity toward achieving a functional family unit. We had to contend with the ugly tentacles of racism, poverty, chemical dependency, and abuse (physical, emotional, and sexual). The prospect of a Black child maturing healthily into adulthood mentally, emotionally, and spiritually under such conditions were very small. I did not want my child to have to endure the burden of poverty, a broken-home, and an onslaught of other things, because of my life's circumstances.

~~~

"Mymomme, what did you call and tell Neeka?" I said angrily into the phone receiver.

"What did she say I said?" Mymomme responded smartly.

"She said that you told her not to have an abortion!"

"Yeah, that's what I said to her."

"And, you don't see nothing wrong with that?"

"No, I don't. She shouldn't have no abortion."

"That's not the issue: the issue is that, after I confided in you, you would go behind my back, and call this girl to tell her not to have an abortion! That's wrong! You betrayed my confidence in you!"

"Well, I don't see it like that!"

"Huh? How can you not? What if you shared some personal information with me and I went and shared it with someone? Wouldn't you feel betrayed?!" I asked, disbelieving that she saw no wrong in her action. "I understand that, if we decide to have our baby, it would be your grandchild, but this is our child! You don't have the right to decide whether we choose to keep him or her! That's our decision!" I continued.

"And, you said to her that she doesn't need me; that she can raise this baby on her own! What mother says that in reference to her son? You act like I'm some horrible person that would leave his child fatherless! I'm looking at Neeka and my circumstances; that I have no means of supporting a child; that my relationship with Neeka isn't healthy; that, if we have this child, he or she will have a grandmother who has called her sons 'fags and bitches' and a grandfather who doesn't even talk to his own children!

I would love to have a child; however, it would be selfish of me to only consider my want of a child. I have to think of my child's quality of life, if he or she is born. Unlike you, I don't choose to think selfishly, as you are clearly only thinking of your want of a grandchild whom is fathered by me."

"Well, I still say she shouldn't have a abortion! Me and yo' daddy didn't have no abortion with you!"

I was livid. I was hurt. I could not believe that Mymomme would talk against me in the manner that she had to LaNeeka. I was the same person who, at thirteen years of age, assumed the responsibility of caring for her one-year-old son, because she had gone to prison for larceny; I was the same person that supported her, listened to her, and encouraged her during her thirty-plus years of physical abuse by her partners and her use of illicit substances; I was the same person who provided a safe home, whereby she could achieve sobriety. Yet, she had betrayed me in an effort to fulfill her vain need to be a grandmother.

"Considering all that I've been through with y'all, you should have strongly considered it!" I replied before I disconnected the call.

~~~

"I spoke with Tiana the other day. She is really maturing into a wonderful, young lady. Did you call her on her birthday?" I asked my daddy.

"No, I didn't call her. She stopped talking me. You don't do that to your father. I don't even know why she's upset, but that's her problem...I sleep well every night," he replied callously into the phone receiver.

Nearly a year before, my sister, Tiana, had stopped talking to my daddy. Her choice to discontinue communicating with him was an accumulation of hurts and disappointments over the years.

"Dad, as I understand the situation, you told the mechanic that all Tiana does is ask you for money. She is upset that you shared personal things about her to a stranger."

"I didn't tell her that!" He stated emphatically. "I don't even know who she's talking about...I bet it's that gay mechanic. She just trying to get something started between Tiana and me!"

My daddy had forgotten that he had already shared the details of the situation with me and that he had stated that he had, in fact, said what Tiana later discovered.

"Well, Tiana is wondering how the girl would know the things, if you hadn't shared them with her."

"I'on know how she knows them, but I ain't gone waste no time trying to figure it out. If she doesn't want to have a relationship with me, that's on her. I ain't gone worry about these kids not wanting to talk to me. Well, I stopped talking to Corey…I just don't like his ways."

"Dad, I think some of this is your responsibility. Remember when you told me that you whooped Tiana when she was a child? Well, she explained the entire situation in greater detail. I didn't know that you had gone to the extremes that you did in disciplining her. Her issue with you isn't just what you said to the mechanic; that was the tip of the iceberg. She is angry and hurt over many of the abusive things that you did to her as well.

As far as Corey is concerned, a lot of his issues are because of you. You kept his birth a secret. He feels like no one knows him in our family, because you didn't acknowledge his existence to our family. And, his step-daddy was mean toward him. I know that Corey's mother loved him, though, because of his step-daddy's actions, he had an emotionally and mentally abusive childhood. And, you didn't help matters by cutting him off and not talking to him when he was only a teenager," I conveyed.

"Well, that's their issues…so, if what you're saying is true, I could blame my issues on Mother."

"Yeah, actually, you can. I'm not saying that Mother wasn't a good mother, because I believe that she was, but she kept your parentage a secret in the same way that you did Corey's. And, I believe her actions have affected you in the same way that your actions have affected Corey."

"Well, I ain't gone accept responsibility for their issues…I ain't got to have a relationship with neither one of them!" He said with finality.

I was incensed. I sat for a long moment processing my daddy's stance regarding his children. I found it hard to believe that he could behave so nonchalantly in matters related to my siblings. His failure as a parent solidified my decision.

Life was filled with uncertainties. Upon our births, none of us was given roadmaps to guide and to direct our steps through life; no road signs to instruct us when to make a right or left turn; no signal lights to tell us to yield, to stop, or to go…

LaNeeka emerged from the inner chambers on stiff legs. Upon seeing her, I quickly rose from my seat in the crowded waiting room. I hugged her firmly before we made our way to my car. Once inside the car, LaNeeka shared with me the horrific details of her experience.

"I wish you could have been back there with me, but the nurse said you couldn't come," she expressed.

"Why not?" I asked.

"I don't know. She said my mother or somebody else could have come back, but not a boyfriend or spouse."

"That's strange," I stated aloud, perplexed by the agency's rules.

"You should have seen her," LaNeeka said, referring to our child.

LaNeeka and I had come to the conclusion that our baby was a girl, because of a dream that I had before we had even known that LaNeeka was pregnant. In the dream, LaNeeka had just given birth to a girl-child.

"Me and the nurse could see her on the monitor moving her little legs! The nurse started laughing, 'cause it looked like she was riding a bike! I told the nurse that she got that from her daddy: always running and working out!" LaNeeka's laughter faded from her voice as the realization of what had just occurred re-entered her consciousness. "I never felt so alone as I did back there in that room by myself," LaNeeka muttered as slow moving tears streamed down her cheeks.

I grabbed LaNeeka's hand in comfort as I turned in my seat to hug her, "I'm sorry. I didn't know what else to do," I offered in sympathy, regarding our decision to abort our baby.

LaNeeka had made the ultimate sacrifice for me; for, while she understood the issues in our lives, she wanted to give birth to our baby. The beauty of her love, respect, and devotion of me pierced through me like a two-edged sword.

I disengaged from our embrace, turning my head toward the window as I sobbed for the loss of our child and the ordeal that LaNeeka had gone through alone. I had prayed fervently for a word from God as to what direction to take. Yet, as the days and weeks progressed, everything had seemed to lead to the termination of my seed on a cold, dreary day in Detroit, Michigan on February 19, 2014.

Chapter Ten

Shortly after the abortion of my child, I moved back to the Atlanta area. Although I grieved the loss of my baby, I felt like I had been given another chance to set things right in my life; an opportunity to start anew. For the first time in my life, I fully understood the consequences that resulted from having unprotected, heterosexual sex.

As a gay person, the greatest fear in my community was of contracting HIV. However, through the conception of my child, I understood that an unplanned or unwanted pregnancy could be equally as frightful for some heterosexuals as was contracting HIV for members of the gay community.

Through my baby's conception, I better understood the positions of irresponsible fathers or mothers. As disheartening as was a person's choice not to parent his child, I knew firsthand what it felt like to have the responsibility of being a father hurled at him as a result of the irresponsibleness of his decision not to protect himself sexually. I also better understood the dysfunction that ensues from having a child under less than wholesome circumstances, i.e. a one-night encounter, teenage sex, or a lack of love between the partners.

Using my own conception as a premise, my parents were essentially children when I was conceived: my mother was seventeen and my father was nineteen years of age. On several occasions my daddy had very candidly expressed to me that he never wanted to father any children. While my dad never directly verbalized his feelings, or lack thereof, about Mymomme, I ascertained from his conversations with me that he did not love her. Mymomme was simply a "girl" whom had a beautiful body and with whom he could copulate. He had no intentions of being in a serious monogamous relationship with her, and he certainly did not intend to have any children with her. Although my daddy very well could have fully accepted the responsibility that resulted from his choice to have unprotected sex with my mother, because of who he was as a person, he could not be anything more than what he was—a part-time father.

Although I made no excuses for the behavior of parents who abdicated the responsibility of parenting their children, I had come to understand that the choice to be a parent to one's child was not as simple as I had assumed it to be. How could a parent wholly love, protect, and care for his offspring when he had none of those feelings for the child's mother? How could a mother fully nourish her child mentally and emotionally when, every time she looked in the eyes of her child, she saw the face of the man whom had scorned her?

My epiphany further allowed me to place in perspective the lack of autonomy that males faced in the birth of their children. Because children are conceived in a female's body, males had no control as to whether their children would live or die; such honors were the choices of females. A male's entire future rested upon the decision of the child-bearer.

As a former incarcerate, the mere thought that another person could determine the course of my life with simply, "Yes, I am going to have my baby" was beyond frightening to me. Upon my release from prison many years prior, I had promised myself that I would never permit anyone to wield the same kind of authority over me as was done during my incarceration; yet, because of the irresponsibleness of my actions, I had given such power to LaNeeka.

~~~

I had shared too much.

Generally, I only divulged the personal matters of my life with Brandy and Geneva. However, my relationship with Brandy was strained and Geneva was gone. While I still loved Brandy deeply, her cantankerous disposition and, at times, her mean-spiritedness had ultimately worn away the fondness that I had once felt for her. After thirteen years of being home from prison, I had finally come to accept that, in some ways, she was not the same person for whom I held a special affinity most of my life.

As a result of my relationship with Brandy having altered and, because of Geneva's death, I was left without a confidant. In my need to share my personal struggles, I turned to Janelle. She was sweet-natured and intelligent, and, in many ways, she reminded me of the Brandy that I remembered as a child.

I placed a very high premium on those in whom I disclosed my innermost thoughts. I had seen far too many people share their deepest feelings with someone, only to have their confidence betrayed or to receive faulty counseling.

I tried to be careful, though sometimes I failed.

"I think Neeka thinks that we're still in a relationship together," I expressed to Janelle as she prepared to leave for work early one morning.

"Yeah, that's 'cause you keep leading her on!" Janelle exclaimed.

"Huh?" I asked bewilderedly.

I was stunned. *'Leading her on!'* What?! I was not an advantageous person. I had never done anything as callously-selfish as to deceive anyone in any manner, especially LaNeeka. I adored her. I knew very few people who had a beautiful spirit like hers—to take advantage or to mislead anyone was coldhearted, yet, the act was even more contemptuous when it was against someone as loving and giving as LaNeeka.

On many occasions, I had attempted to fully sever my relationship with LaNeeka; though, each time I did so, my efforts had ended disastrously with LaNeeka crying uncontrollably and appearing to be on the verge of a mental/emotional breakdown.

While I knew that I could not assume total responsibility for LaNeeka's well-being, I simply did not have whatever it took to entirely cut all ties with her. LaNeeka had done no true wrong toward me; she had not committed an offense against me. She simply was not the person I wanted as my partner. Had she done the same things to me as my previous partners, the decision not to have her in my life would have been easy for me, but she had not. As such, I saw no reason why we could not maintain a friendship with one another.

"I..I..gotta go to work!" Janelle said exasperatedly, as she opened the front door of her apartment. "I'll call you when I get to work," she expressed in her sweet, honey-laced voice.

As Janelle gently shut the front door behind herself, I quietly closed-off my need to share my thoughts and feelings with her regarding the intimate details of my life.

~~~~

Corey and I decided to sublease the apartment below Janelle's. Susan, the occupant of the apartment, had to rush back home to Texas to be with her boyfriend whose mother was ill with cancer.

Subleasing the apartment was an ideal arrangement for all of us involved: Susan's credit was salvaged; and, Corey and I had a place of our own for several months while we looked for another home.

Sharing an apartment with Corey was somewhat of a dream come true. I had always wondered what it would be like to be single and to date precariously. Having been incarcerated during most of my twenties, I did not have the luxury of getting to know different people and choosing from amongst the best of them to whom to give my heart. Instead, I went from relationship to relationship, falling in love along the way, without ever quite finding the person of my dreams.

With my younger brother as my housemate and friend, I intended to live my life differently than I had in previous years. In my mind, I envisioned Corey and I having small, social gatherings in our apartment amongst friends and acquaintances; we would imbibe until were in a drunken-stupor; then, with an entourage of friends accompanying us to a popular nightclub, each of us would happen upon delectable mates with whom we would have unadulterated sex.

While the image in my head was tantalizing, it fell very short of our reality. There were no lavish, liquor-laden house parties, followed by festive ventures to exquisite nightclubs—though in place of the former two, my brother and I did have unbridled sex with our respective partners. During the first two months of our stay in the apartment, I had sexual escapades with five different guys—more partners than I had in any one year, let alone two months.

Yet, with every unchecked inhibition, a huge duty oftentimes accompanies.

"Hey, bro! What you doin'?" Corey asked.

"Hey, bae! Not much…up here in Nelle's apartment gettin' fucked up!" I laughed.

"Ahhh, y'all drinkin' already?" He asked.

"Yes, sir! Nelle made me some kinda drink, and I mean it is on point! You heard me?!" I asked jokingly.

"Well, save a little for me! I'm on my way! Oh, and I'm bringing a friend with me. I want you to meet him."

"Okay, I'll see you in a bit," I responded as we disconnected the call.

Moments later, Corey walked in Janelle's apartment with a tall, slender, light-skinned guy.

"Hey, bae!" I greeted Corey as soon as I saw him enter the apartment. On distrustful legs, I stood to hug him.

"Heeeey!" Corey replied as he returned my hug. "This is my friend, Jason," Corey said as he turned to the guy beside him. To Jason, "Jason, this my big brother, Chris."

"Hey, Jason. Good to meet you," I said in a deep, alcohol-burdened voice as Jason and I shook hands.

One could have called me stupid, naïve, a fool, a damn fool, a drunken fool, or whatever other kind of word that could have come to a person's mind to describe my behavior, but the obvious was not so obvious to me at the time.

"You want somethin' to drink? Corey ain't go hardly drink nothin'! Him and Nelle will smoke the house down, but they ain't gone take nothin' but a couple of sips of a good ass drink?" I asked Jason.

I had drunk way too much. I was garrulous by nature, though rarely was I so talkative with people whom I had just met.

"Yeah, I'll have whatever you havin'…apparently it's good!" Nelle, her girlfriend, Corey and I laughed at Jason's remark.

"Well, Nelle made this for me, but I'll do my best to make one like it for you! Pray for me, 'cause I ain't good at making no drinks!"

I wobbled from the kitchen after I had prepared Jason's drink.

"Here you go," I said to Jason as I handed him the drink.

I plopped close to Jason on the sofa, perhaps a little too closely. While the five of us engaged in good-humored conversation, I took every chance I could to flirt with Jason. As things continued to escalate between Jason and me, I leaned over to kiss him; however, before my lips could meet his, he quickly placed his outstretched palms on my shoulders, stopping me within a few inches of his mouth. I smiled at him mischievously. Then, without warning, he relaxed his arms, until our lips met one another's.

"Cousin Chris, what is goin' on with you?!" Janelle exclaimed from the dining table where she sat in front of Jason and me.

With a look of delight, I smugly sat back on the sofa, "I'on know…blame it on the aaaaaalcohol," I smiled innocently.

Everyone, save Jason, was surprised by my behavior. It was as though another person had taken my body and mind! I did not even like to kiss, particularly strangers—and the guy was not my type! I preferred thick-built, dark-skinned guys! Jason was thin and light-skinned!

As the evening came to an end, I turned to Jason, "You staying downstairs with me?"

Apparently, my obnoxious, flirtatious behavior had won Jason's affection, "I can't. I have to go to work in the morning, but you can take me home."

"Awww, what? Who works on a Saturday morning, anymore?!"

"Me!" Janelle quipped from the kitchen.

"Ahhhh, okay!" I bemoaned humorously. "Come on. I'll take you home, then."

After I went downstairs to get my keys from my apartment, Jason and I got into my Camaro.

"You got to tell me where to go, 'cause I don't know how to get to your spot. I'm still learning all these different hoods in Atlanta."

"Okay."

I was actually far too intoxicated to drive, but without making use of good sense, I started my car and drove to Jason's apartment; and, thankfully, we arrived unscathed.

Once inside, Jason escorted me to his bedroom where I quickly undressed and fell into a deep slumber until the sun began to peak through the window blinds a couple of hours later.

"Oh, shit!" I nearly shouted, "You've got to go to work!" I rushed to put on my clothes as fast as I could, albeit still very much inebriated.

"No, I don't. I called off," Jason responded sensually.

"Well, I got to go to my daddy's place. I forgot I told him that I would check on it while he is gone out-of-town."

"Can I go with you?" Jason asked.

"I'on care."

Jason and I arrived at my daddy's house a few short minutes after leaving his apartment. As soon as I entered my daddy's apartment, I hurriedly shed my clothes and hopped onto the bed and beneath the comforter.

"I gotta sleep off this alcohol. My head is spinning. The remote is right there, if you want to watch T.V." I offered.

Within seconds, I was asleep. I awakened to the feeling of drums beating within my scull. I grabbed the throbbing temples of my head, massaging them tenderly in hopes of relieving the tension; yet, the band persisted, despite the heartiest of my attempts to quiet it.

I rose from the bed and tried to raise my arms to stretch my aching muscles; however, the effort made the pounding in my head more severe. Instead, I twisted to my right side, catching a glimpse of the sleeping frame.

Oh, my God! The night's adventure rushed into my sobering consciousness! Oh, my God! Oh, my God! I repeated over and over in my mind as the details of the previous evening pushed its way into reality.

I looked to the right once more to get another glimpse of the sleeping man. Oh, my God! He was light-skinned! *Oh, shit!* I looked at him once more. *Oh, no!!!* His nose was rather large! *Shit...shit...shit!!!* He had pimples on his face! I did not need to look any further, but I did so just to cause more agony to myself and to confirm what I already knew...damn...damn...damn! He was skinny!

Fuuuck! I thought as I took note of what the guy's physical features meant, then, "Shit!" I unconsciously spoke aloud, waking him.

"Hey," he said, groggily.

I wasted no time. "Good morning...are you and Corey dating?"

"Uh, no," he replied, looking perplexed.

Jason. That is his name, I remembered. I looked at him once more as I grabbed my cell phone to text Corey.

"Are you sure? Did y'all fuck around or anything?" I asked Jason.

I already knew the answers to my questions. The truth was written all over Jason's face and body. He was light-skinned, small-framed, and, although he was not unattractive, he was slightly 'funny-looking'—all qualities that Corey liked in his men.

I quickly texted Corey: 'Oh, my God! Corey, why didn't you tell me?!'

Corey: 'Tell you what?'

Me: 'That you and this boy had messed around; that y'all like each other!'

Corey: 'It ain't that serious; nothing happened. We just cool.'

"Yea, a long time ago we did. Why?" Jason replied as Corey and I were texting.

Me: 'Yes, y'all did, Corey. He just told me…I'm so sorry! Why didn't you say something?!'

Corey: 'It's cool. You know how these queens are: they see somebody else and they forget you.'

"Oh, my God! I knew it! I can't believe this! Why didn't y'all say something to me?!" I asked of Jason.

"Say something about what?" Jason asked naively.

The generations of eighties and nineties were something else to me! They did everything under the sun without any remorse at all as to their behavior!

"What do you mean?! Say that you and my brother are dating!" I queried incredulously.

"But, we're not dating."

"Datin…fuckin…whatever y'all doing or did, y'all should have said something! Corey should have said something! Fuck!" I exclaimed as I put my head in my hands, "And, I kissed you. Shit! Shit! Shit! I didn't know…He should have told me…I should have known. You look just like the type of guys that he likes! Damn!" I said miserably. I felt absolutely awful.

"We're not dating, though. I don't even like him like that."

"You must've liked him…y'all fucked around!" I snapped. "And, even if you don't like him, he likes you!" I fumed as I further realized that I allowed this guy who cares nothing about my brother to hurt him.

I was thoroughly disappointed with myself. I could not believe that I had done something so horrible to Corey, unknowingly or not.

~~~

"Chris, come here," LaNeeka whispered to me from my bedroom.

"Huh?" I asked once we were inside the darkened room.

"I heard Corey say he like that guy you like," LaNeeka continued to whisper conspiratorially.

LaNeeka and I had managed to maintain a deep, abiding friendship with one another after the abortion of our baby.

"Huh? Who you talking about?" I asked.

"Donny; that one guy you said you like."

"How you know he like him?"

"'Cause I heard him talking to Tiana about him. He musta thought I was sleep…I heard him say, 'Ralph cool, but too bad, I like his best friend.'"

"Hmmm," I pondered LaNeeka's revelation.

I did not know what to make of the information that LaNeeka shared with me. I met Donny while attending a house party with Corey. Ralph, a guy that Corey was dating at the time, shared an apartment with Donny. Weeks prior, Corey had mentioned that he thought Donny was cute, but I thought nothing of his comment, since his relationship with Ralph had begun to gain momentum; though, apparently, if what LaNeeka said was true, Corey still desired Donny, despite his courtship with Ralph.

In spite of my attraction toward Donny, I had resolved not to pursue anything with him. I did not want to have a situation like the one I had with Jason; though, later that evening, I received a text message from an unknown number.

Unknown Texter: Hello there, sir.

Me: Hey. Who is this?

Unknown Texter: Donny (photo attached).

Me: Oh, what's up, baby?

Donny: Not much. How are you? Hope u don't mind. I solicited your number lol

Me: I'm well…np (no problem). I actually asked Corey to give you my number. I presume you didn't get the message.

Donny: No, I got it, but I had told him that I want urs (yours) awhile ago.

Me: Oh, he didn't tell me.

Donny's text message left me feeling uneasy with Corey. Rather than to allow ill-feelings to reside in my spirit against Corey, I decided to confront him about the situation.

"Do you mind if I say something to Corey about what you shared with me?" I asked LaNeeka.

She took a moment to think for several seconds before she responded to my question, "Uhm, no, I don't mind…"

"Okay. I don't like how he handled this thing with Donny…I mean, Donny is cool. He's a good looking guy, but it ain't that serious. Corey didn't have to deliberately try to keep us from one another. I don't care about these dudes like that, unless I'm in a relationship with the guy; otherwise, fuck them. Corey acts like my friend, Erin. He's like pressed about these niggas and most of them ain't worth losing no sleep over."

An hour or so later, Corey arrived home.

"Corey, I need to talk to you," I said to him as he passed through the living room en route to the kitchen.

"Okay," he replied nervously.

"Neeka said that she overheard you talking to Tiana about liking Donny."

"Huh? I didn't say that. She musta heard me wrong…I don't like him…Me and Tiana wasn't even talking about him," Corey replied agitatingly.

"No, she said that she specifically heard you referring to Donny, because you mentioned him by name." I countered.

"Uhn uh, she don't know what she talking about…she wasn't even here when me and Tiana was talking."

"Actually, she was; she was in my bedroom lying down trying to go to sleep when she heard you say what you said…anyway, it doesn't make a difference. Donny texted me. He said that he asked you to give me his number and that you had never given him my number as I asked you to do weeks ago."

"He lying. He never asked me to give you his number," Corey responded defensively.

"Well, why didn't you give him my number as I had asked of you?" I did not wait for him to respond before I continued, "I'm telling you Corey, you act a lot like Erin. He was very jealous-hearted and territorial when it came to these dudes. You need to stop placing so much energy into these dudes. Niggas come a dime a dozen; they're plentiful. And, most of them ain't worth the time of day."

"I got other nice looking friends. We all nice looking. Stosha always get attention. I'm cool with it," Corey interjected.

Sometimes one has to say very little for the truth of a person's feelings to be revealed. I had never said anything to Corey about attractiveness or about getting attention; yet, his Freudian slip revealed much about his inner thoughts.

Donny and I entertained one another very briefly through a few phone conversations and an occasional exchange of text messages. I soon learned that Donny was heavily involved in a romantic relationship while he was in pursuit of me...

...And, just like that, the appeal of dating various guys and having indiscriminate sex was gone. I quickly settled back into my conservative ways.

~~~~

As was my usual, I was awake late into the evening hours and well into the early morning thumbing through the many profiles on a gay chat site when my phone chimed, an indication that I had received a message from someone on the site.

"Hi," a guy saluted me; I responded in kind.

I looked at his profile: his posted photo only revealed his body from the neck down, which I did not mind. I was drawn toward bodies, not faces.

I liked what I saw: flat abs, thick legs, nicely toned chest and arms. He listed his statistics as 5'11, 175lbs. *Nice*. I liked men who were slightly taller and heavier than me. I continued to read his profile: Twenty-five-years-old!

Although I was not necessarily looking to find love through the chat app, I was not expecting to entertain someone twenty-five years old, either! He was way too young for me! I had my fair share of dealings with young people. I was absolutely not interested in having a relationship with another one on any level, whether as a friend, lover, or foe.

Contrary to my recent history, I did not like to date young people. Even as a teenager, I had been attracted to older people. I loved maturity, and I relished in the opportunity to learn something new. While I firmly believed that a person could learn from anyone, regardless of the person's age, I seldom found the lessons that accompanied young people very interesting. Yet, for reasons that were not clear to me, young people seemed to gravitate to me. Perhaps, they were like me during my youth; fascinated by the mature sophistication of an older guy.

I did not know where the guy's interest lay; however, our conversation was interesting enough for us to exchange phone numbers and to make plans to meet in person the following day.

~~~

Our plans were sabotaged. After texting him during the afternoon, I received grave news.

"GM (good morning), E-R-I-K!" I made certain to spell his name correctly. When he had initially given me his phone number, my phone autocorrected the spelling of his name to read: Eric, with a "C". Before I could change the mishap, he quickly texted the correct spelling in bold letters.

"Good morning," he replied.

"How are you?" I asked.

"Not too good. My grandfather passed away this morning. I have to fly out to Texas in a few hours."

"Oh, wow! I'm sorry to hear that. My granddaddy passed away a few years ago, so I know the feeling of losing a grandfather. I know that we don't know each other, but, if there is anything that I can do to help you, if you want to talk or anything, I'm here," I stated.

"Thanks! I appreciate that!"

"No problem...I'll let you go. I know you probably have to pack and stuff. Again, I'm sorry for your loss."

"Thanks. I'll text you soon…just gotta make travel arrangements."

"Okay. Take your time. I'm here."

As strange as it may have been, the death of Erik's grandfather formed a connection with me for him. As a result of my own personal experiences with death; specifically, losing a grandfather, I felt a kinship of sorts with Erik. Although I did not know Erik, I bonded with him in his grief.

~~~

Days passed by quickly. Erik flew to his home-state of Texas to be with his family during his time of loss. After his grandfather had been laid to rest, Erik flew to Chicago to fulfill a three-month long internship.

With each passing day, Erik and I learned more and more about one another. The more I learned about him, the more impressed I became. Early on, during our exchanges, Erik had shared with me that he was a college student. I had assumed that he was working toward achieving his bachelor's degree. I was wrong: he was in pursuit of a master's degree, and not just any master's degree. His degree was in divinity.

I usually did not place a lot of importance in college degrees. While I recognized the societal value and the hard work that was required to achieve a college degree, I was not overly impressed with degrees or a bunch of letters behind ones' name, i.e. M.S., M.A., LPC, LSW, D.N., etc. Although I valued education, years of living had shown me that a college degree was not always indicative of intellect. I knew far too many individuals who were armed with college degrees, yet they did not have the intelligence of a field mouse. Conversely, I knew many persons who had never stepped a toe on a college campus; however, they had the knowledge of a hundred professors.

Still, Erik's pursuit of a graduate degree impressed me. I was awed by his endeavor to achieve the degree for several different reasons: his age, the discipline that he chose, and his socioeconomic status. While I knew there were many students who pursued graduate degrees shortly after accomplishing their bachelor's degree, I did not know of many Black students who embarked upon such a challenge, and I definitely did not anyone who chose to pursue a graduate degree in theology.

In fact, I had never had a personal relationship with anyone who sought a degree in theology, let alone a young, African American person of twenty-five years of age. In addition to Erik's academic endeavors, he had come from very humble beginnings. He had been reared in abject poverty; yet, rather than to allow his circumstances as a poor person to cripple him, he used his experiences to propel him toward success.

~~~

The summer was going well for me. I had begun working for Erica, again. She and I had moved pass our past issues as though nothing had ever occurred. I was grateful to her for the opportunity to allow me to work. I had not realized how much I missed going to work each morning.

I also had completed my second autobiography, *He Told Me*. The accomplishment was bittersweet for me. I loved the creative process that writing involved; however, writing the details of my life was heart-wrenching. It pained me to dredge through and to relive the painful experiences that I had placed behind me; yet, I deduced, if I could help someone by sharing my story, the pain was worth enduring.

~~~

I had not been in communication with Mymomme in over six months. However, on Father's Day, she left a voice message with me asking for forgiveness. Although I had not completely healed from her act of betrayal, I returned her phone call.

"Hey there," I greeted.

"Hey, bae," Mymomme responded on the other end of the receiver.

"What are you up to?" I asked.

"Awww, nothing. Just getting home from church."

"Ah, nice. How was it?"

"It was all right, you know."

"Good. How is the pastor?"

"He doing good. You know his new wife go to the church now?"

"Yeah, I think you told me that she was a member there."

"Mmm, okay. What you doing for your birthday?"

"I don't know exactly, yet, but my daddy's side of my family is talking about going to Myrtle Beach. I was going to see if Sherelle wanted to go with me since it's his birthday, too. It'll give him the opportunity to see another state," I replied.

At nearly thirteen years of age, I thought it was a good time to expose my nephew to different regions of the country. Traveling broadened one's mind and it would allow Sherelle to see a part of the world that existed beyond the confines of Toledo.

"Aw, yeah, that'll be nice…I think he'll enjoy that…"

"Yeah, I think he will, too…" A part of me did not want to ask, but I did not want to be rude toward Mymomme, either. "You want to come with us, if we do decide to go?" I asked.

"Mmmm, yeah, I'd love to. You know, De-De go down there every year for the biker thang."

Oh, no!!! I did not expect Mymomme to accept my offer! I did not know whether I was ready to have such intimate dealings with her. I felt that I needed more time to heal. Each time that Mymomme did something to violate our relationship, I had forgiven and accepted her back into my life with open arms. While I was sincere in my forgiveness, I had grown weary of going through the same things over and over again with her.

Though, since I had extended the invite, it would be mean of me to rescind it.

"Okay, I'll keep you posted on whether we go or not."

"Okay, bae."

I really did not know who awakened me. It could have been the Holy Spirit, though it also could have been the spirit of the adversary. All I knew was: I was sleeping very peacefully in a deep, deep slumber when I suddenly rose from the bed as though someone had yanked me upward by my neck. I awakened just in the nick of time to overhear her.

"Yea…it was shit! He left it there!" She said angrily.

That was all I heard. And, just as quickly as I had awakened, I went back to sleep. The experience seemed more like a dream than reality; however the event, or actually the event that preceded it, would change my interactions with Janelle for years to come.

"Janelle, are you okay?" I asked after I walked into her apartment and into her bedroom.

I knew that she was not okay, however, I wanted her to say that she was not okay, rather than talking to others about the situation and avoiding me.

"Yes, I'm okay. Why?"

"The other day I heard you outside of my bedroom window talking to someone about me leaving shit in your apartment."

"Yea, I did," Janelle said wearily.

In some ways, I felt sympathy for her. She was overwhelmed: she had a full-time job and she was essentially a single parent, as she and her husband were separated and raising their daughters primarily rested on Janelle. Since her separation from her husband, she had entered a romantic relationship with a woman. The relationship, coupled with maintaining her other responsibilities, was mentally and emotionally draining for her.

"Well, if you had a problem with what happened, why didn't you just say something to me?"

"I don't know…I was too upset to say anything…I just know, when I came home, it was shit all over my apartment—in the living room, the hallway, on the walls."

"Well, when I got there to take him for a walk, the dog had already shitted in the kitchen."

"So, you just left the shit there?"

"Yes, I did. Nelle, I told you to stop over-feeding the dog, because that is what happens. He did the same thing the two other times you overfed him and I had to clean his cage and the kitchen floor where he shitted."

"I just wish you had told me you had a problem with taking him out."

"I didn't and don't have a problem with taking him outside."

"Well, Corey said you didn't like taking the dog out."

"Listen, Corey, don't know what he talkin' about. If I didn't want to take the dog out, I wouldn't. I took it upon myself to take the dogs for walks. You didn't ask me to do that."

Janelle had taken on more responsibility than she could bear. The dog actually belonged to her girlfriend, however, when she and her girlfriend began to have problems in their relationship, her girlfriend moved back to her home state of New York where she cared for her elderly aunt. Janelle offered to care for the dog during her girlfriend's absence, though Janelle did not have the financial resources or the time to care for the dog, as she was away from home for long hours working double-shifts.

"I just didn't like coming home to seeing shit everywhere!"

"Well, I'm sorry he shit all over your place, but I wasn't cleaning it, again. I don't like messing with human shit, let alone shit from a dog. And, I kept telling you not to give the dog too much food. As soon as I took him outside to walk, he literally shitted right outside of the apartment building door, then we walked to that tree, not even fifteen feet from where he had just shitted and he shitted again! As God is my witness, he shitted at least five times before I finished taking him for a walk!"

Janelle did not have a lot of money. At times, she ran out of dog food and the dog would go two to three days without eating. Janelle's way of compensating for her neglect was by giving the dog twice as much food during the times when she was able to provide for him. Though, the outcome was always disastrous—he would overeat and ultimately defecate in the house.

"Well, you could've just told me that you didn't want to take him out and I could've asked Corey or somebody to take him!"

I laughed exasperatedly. "I'm telling you, I don't have a problem taking the dog out. I don't care what Corey's manipulative ass told you, and he really don't want to take the dog out his damn self! He the same one who said he don't like going to your apartment and Lisa's cause y'all got dogs! Now, his two-faced ass actin like he cool with taking the dog out! Talking about he got to take allergy medicine before he come to see y'all! And, no, I'm not going to continue to clean up no dog shit, after I have repeatedly told you not to overfeed him!"

I seriously felt that some people were not meant to have dogs, no matter how much they professed to love them. Pets were a responsibility, not just something to have to ease the void of loneliness or to offer as playmates for children. I knew far too many dog owners that left their dogs in dog-cages while they went to work for eight to nine hours a day!

I was not a "dog-lover," but I had enough sense to know that it was a cruel to leave a dog in a cage for hours upon hours. Many of us humans did not like to be indoors all day, let alone confined to a small room or cage, so why would an animal want to be caged, especially an animal that was created to live outdoors amongst nature?

It was because of my mentality that I took various family members' dogs for walks. I felt that it was important for dogs to walk, not only for cardio-vascular health, but also to sniff things, which was apparently very important to them, because every dog that I had ever taken for walks smelled every tree, fire hydrant, and stop sign that I allowed them to sniff.

~~~~

Two weeks prior to my birthday, I drove to Chicago. It was my second time having gone there to see him. As with the time before, I thoroughly enjoyed myself. Yet, nothing had prepared me for what I witnessed with my very own eyes!

I skirted around the side of bed where I had slept as I made my way to the bathroom. After showering, I exited the bathroom, as I did so I looked out of the corner of my eye to the left. *What! I know he did not!*

I unpretentiously walked around to the other side of the king-sized bed to retrieve my clothes from my gym bag. After getting them, I scanned the floor for the bath towel that I carelessly discarded beside the bed the previous night. It was gone.

As I dried the remainder of the remnants of water from my body, I scanned the room: the pizza box and juice containers that Erik and I had left on the desk were all placed neatly in the wastebasket beside the desk. I was stunned.

The fact that I valued cleanliness was not news to me. Mymomme was obsessive about orderliness; quite naturally, she passed the value onto my brother and me. However, it was not until Erik and I awakened together in a small hotel room in Chicago that I realized just how much I wanted the trait to be exemplified in a partner, or a "potential" partner.

Although none of my past partners were particularly nasty, none of them was as conscious of disorder as was Erik. Mere words could not have expressed how elated I was to discover that I was involved with someone who placed meticulousness on the same plateau as me!

~~~

LaNeeka, Mymomme, Sherelle, and Donraye (my niece) rode together in Mymomme's car to Atlanta. After they arrived to Atlanta, I assumed the responsibility of driving us to Myrtle Beach, South Carolina.

We were all excited. None of us had ever been to Myrtle Beach. I longed to be near the ocean. When I had lived in Long Beach, California, I walked along the beach nearly every night. I loved the scent of the saltwater and the refreshing breeze as it gently caressed my skin. My soul yearned to hear the melody of the ocean's surf.

We arrived in Myrtle Beach shortly after noon; however, after battling traffic, it was nearly three o'clock when we finally reached the oceanfront.

The children leapt from the car in barely contained anticipation of getting in the water. Ordinarily, I did not like to be in the hot sun; yet, deprivation had created an anxious impatience in me. I hurriedly removed my shirt and shoes and ran toward the water like a child running to a candy store!

My family and I delighted in the warmth of the sun and the coolness of the ocean for an hour or so before we met my other family at their hotel suite.

After we had greeted everyone at the hotel, LaNeeka and I quickly left the hotel to explore the city. Myrtle Beach was exquisite. It looked very much like the tourist conglomerate that it was; however, with the Atlantic Ocean, carnival rides, and grand hotels as its backdrop, it was wondrous! I had been told that there were several wonderful restaurants in the area that served delicious seafood. Unfortunately, LaNeeka and I opted against eating at any of the many seafood buffets in the area; instead, we chose to dine on fried, coconut shrimp and salmon from a well-known franchised steakhouse.

~~~

A difference in the temperaments of my family could be felt the moment that LaNeeka and I returned to my family's suite after we had explored the city. They were not rude, though I could not say that they were welcoming, either. We did not know what had transpired during our absence, though it was obvious to us that something had occurred.

LaNeeka and I wondered if, perhaps, they felt that we had stayed gone too long. Yet, rather than to attempt to harness the skills of clairvoyance, Mymomme, LaNeeka, the children, and I left to find a hotel room of our own. Though, try as we did, we were unsuccessful. Everything in close proximity and within a reasonable price was booked.

After an hour had passed, we finally located a hotel with vacancy; however, the hotel was located in Florence, an hour and a half from the city. We decided to stay at the hotel in Florence and to return at noon to join my family in Myrtle Beach, though, by the time morning came, none of us was interested in the long ride back to Myrtle Beach, and so we returned to Atlanta.

We arrived in Atlanta during the early evening. For some reason, Mymomme was in a foul mood. I did not have the energy, or the desire, to give any attention to whatever could have caused her disposition.

"Hey. We gone leave in the morning. Where you want us to sleep at tonight?" Mymomme asked.

"Y'all can sleep in my bedroom. I'll make a pallet on the floor for the kids…Neeka is going to stay here with me and catch the bus back to Toledo."

"How I'm supposed to get back?!" She exclaimed.

"What do you mean? Initially, when I first suggested that she ride with you here to Atlanta, you said that you didn't need her to come, and that you and Sherelle could get here by y'all selves. Now, you saying you need her to take you back home? I wasn't gone say nothing, but since you brought up how you were going to get home: Neeka told me that you were mean to her on the way down here; that she drove well over ninety per cent of the way here and that you were hollering at her while she was driving."

"Hmpf, well, to tell the truth, I ain't feelin' her!"

"What?! You ain't feelin' her?! That girl ain't did nothin' to you! And, if you ain't feelin' her, why would you allow her to come down here with you? She could have caught the bus here! And, why would you even want somebody that you 'ain't feelin' to drive you all the way back to Toledo?! If I ain't feelin' somebody, I leave them alone! I don't ask or expect them to do things for me!"

"I was tellin' Brandy about the baby and how she had a abortion…I figured you told her."

I quickly pounced on Mymomme's comment about my baby. "I didn't tell Bran nothing about the details of our abortion. I don't even talk to her about stuff like that no more!"

"Oh, I didn't know…"

I interrupted her before she could finish her sentence, "And, why would you talk to her about my baby?! She ain't got nothin' to do with my child, and truthfully speaking, you don't, either! That baby was mine and Neeka, not yours! I understand that you lonely and looking to fill the void in your life with a grandchild, but you can't do that with me and mine. I did what I thought was best for me, Neeka, and our baby! And, here you treatin' this girl like a piece of garbage, 'cause she aborted HER child, not YOURS, but HERS! That's the craziest stuff I have ever heard of!" I said as I walked from the living room toward the bedrooms.

A nagging feeling in my spirit had told me not to invite Mymomme to join us in Myrtle Beach. I knew her well. However, not having extended an invitation to her would have plagued me day and night; after all, she was my mother.

I had wondered what Mymomme and Brandy were talking about so intently after LaNeeka and I returned to the beach. I had pushed aside my gut feeling that something was amiss; instead, I assigned the intimacy of their conversation to their long-standing relationship. For, although Mymomme was not Brandy's biological aunt, she had babysat Brandy before I was even born; so, in some ways, she was like an aunt to Brandy.

Mymomme's conversation with Brandy was not the whole of the situation—the tale continued. As I walked back toward my bedroom, I heard the front door open. It was Janelle. She went into Corey's room, had a verbal exchange with him, and then re-entered the living room. As she opened the door to go back upstairs to her apartment, I heard Mymomme express in a malicious whisper, "Now, she say she stayin' here with him and catchin' the bus back. Hmpf," she scoffed right before Janelle closed the front door.

I was incensed! She had come down south with her twisted thoughts and waged a campaign against LaNeeka for having aborted our baby! A child that was incubated within LaNeeka's womb! How dare her! One would have thought that LaNeeka was carrying her unborn child! And, to make matters worse, she had involved my family in her contemptuous, diabolical plan! I suddenly understood why my family had acted so bizarrely in Myrtle Beach.

Without missing a beat, I quickly marched into the living room, "Listen, you can include whoever you want in this mess that has nothing to do with you or them! I can't believe you! What kind of a mother would come all the way out-of-town to her child's home and do this?! You haven't changed a bit! You are still the same mean-spirited woman that you've always been!" I said in disgust as I walked back to my bedroom.

"Sherelle, y'all get y'all stuff and come on!" Mymomme shouted from the living to my nephew and niece.

Within minutes, they had packed their things into Mymomme's car and were gone en route to Toledo.

After Mymomme left, I called Brandy. I wanted to know why she had not shared with me the conversation Mymomme had with her; however, she did not answer the phone. I left a message on her voicemail, asking that she call me upon receipt of my message.

Chapter Eleven

I was in-lust with him after I first saw his photos; I was in-like with him after our first phone conversation; I was in-love with him long before he entered the Georgian state-line.

Erik's internship had finally ended in Chicago. After a long-awaited three months, he was back in Atlanta to continue his studies at Emory University. I was ecstatic to have him home. I had dreamed of us dining at luxurious restaurants, taking long walks in Piedmont Park under the brilliance of a moonlit sky, making passionate love until our bodies were drenched in warm sweat and unbridled ecstasy, and sharing our hearts' desires until the sandman worked his charm—my dream had come true. We did all those things and many, many more; yet, just three short weeks after Erik's return to Atlanta, the honeymoon came to an end.

I awakened late in the morning to the sound of Erik's voice coming from the direction of the living room. I shielded my eyes from the radiance of the sun that sifted through the window blinds. I arched my back, stretching long and hard before I rose from the bed. I felt wonderful. I could not remember the last time that I had slept so soundly. Erik's foam mattress suited my deeply arched back well.

After urinating and washing my hands, I walked back into Erik's bedroom to make his bed. For the past week, I had been spending my nights at his place. The decision to stay overnight at his home gave us the opportunity to sleep and awaken next to one another.

Just after I had pulled the comforter over the sheets and fluffed the pillows, Erik entered the room.

"I just got off the phone with my doctor at school. My test results came back positive for Chlamydia…Hold on…That's probably the doctor's office calling me back."

I stood numbly at the side of Erik's bed in shock. Although I had sex with several persons prior to my relationship with Erik, I had gone to the clinic and was given a clean bill of health, though, something was obviously wrong.

The last person with whom I had been sexually involved was a Brazilian guy named Marco. Although Marco and I had practiced safe sex in the beginning of our relationship, I did not use a condom the last time that I penetrated him.

I had to have contracted Chlamydia from Marco, I pondered...but he had told me that he tested negative of any STIs (sexually transmitted infections), including HIV, and I had not had sex with anyone else in the past three months, other than Erik and him.

I paced throughout Erik's bedroom as I thought long and hard about my dilemma.

I had terminated my courtship with Marco at the near start of my involvement with Erik, when I knew that my feelings for Erik were becoming serious. Perhaps, I had not ended things quickly enough, or maybe I had sex with Erik too soon.

I hastily grabbed my phone from the desk in Erik's room to call Marco, though, instead of speaking with him, I was received his voicemail.

"A, Marco, this is Chris. The guy that I told you I was in a relationship with just told me that he tested positive for Chlamydia. I know it's been awhile since we last had sex, but you're the last person that I had sex with. I think you should get yourself tested."

After disconnecting the call, I went into the bathroom to take a quick shower. Once I finished showering, I quickly put on my clothes and entered the living room where Erik sat on the sofa in deep thought.

"I'm about to go to the clinic to get tested. What did the doctor say?" I asked.

"He said that all the test came back negative, except the one for Chlamydia. They gave me a oral and a anal test. The anal test came back positive for Chlamydia."

"Hmmm," I responded as I began to think. "I called Marco, the dude that I said I was messing around with before you and I got in a relationship, to tell him what's going on. He texted me back expressing that he was at work, but he stated that he is negative of any STDs, so I'm going to the clinic to see what they say. When did you say you last had sex prior to me?"

"In April with Josh," Erik replied.

"And, y'all had protected sex?" I queried.

"Yes...Let's see, I didn't have sex when I went to Texas for my grandfather's funeral...I didn't have sex in Chicago...yea, Josh, is the last person that I had sex with," Erik expressed absentmindedly as he thought of his past sexual partners.

"Hmmm, okay. We'll I'm about to head to the clinic. I'll hit you up when I leave there," I said.

"Okay. I'm going to call the doctor again to see how long a person can have Chlamydia in their body."

"All right."

~~~

While at the clinic, I asked the technician for a record of my last test results. He obliged. As I knew, I was given a full examination: oral, anal, and blood. All of the tests yielded negative results, and, furthermore, I was tested after Marco and I last had sex. Yet, I requested to be re-tested and to be given an antibiotic shot to kill any possible trace of the disease.

Three days later, I received a phone call from the clinic with the results of my most recent examination. As with before, the tests results were negative; I did not have any sexually transmitted diseases.

"I spoke with the technician from the clinic. He said that my results were negative for Chlamydia, syphilis, gonorrhea, and HIV. I couldn't have given you Chlamydia. Tell me again about your experience with Josh?" I asked Erik calmly.

"They probably made a mistake with your results. I was tested at Emory. I know my results are accurate. Didn't you say that you went to a public clinic?" Erik asked haughtily.

I laughed aloud at the absurdity of his statement. "So, you're saying that because I was tested at a public clinic and, since you were tested at the 'world-renown' Emory, your results are more accurate than mine?"

"Well, yeah, Emory University has an excellent hospital…"

"Yeah, yeah, yeah, you don't have to give me the spiel about Emory's reputation," I said, interrupting Erik's rants about Emory. After weeks of courtship, I had soon realized that Erik's self-worth was attached to him attending Emory. While Emory was a great school and I was proud of him for attending it, I had learned long ago that true self-worth had to come from within a person and that it should not be attached to something as mundane as a university that one attended. "I'm well-aware of it. You need to get off of your high-horse and accept that you didn't get this disease from me and, since you didn't get it from me, we need to find out when and with whom you got it. Now, you said that the last time you had sex was in April?"

"Yeah," Erik responded apprehensively.

"So, that means that you've had Chlamydia for the past five months."

"Yeah, I guess."

"Well, if you did, in fact, get it from this guy, Josh, five months ago, y'all had to have had unprotected sex," I persisted.

"Well…one time…he did tell me that he had a fetish…"

"A fetish for what?" I inquired.

"He said that when he cums he likes to take off his condom and nut on the dude's ass."

"What? So, you saying that this dude just nutted on your ass?! Naw, I don't believe that. I been fucking way too long to go for some shit like that! He had to have put his dick in you! Did he fuck you without the condom?!"

"Yeah," Erik responded quietly.

"So, you telling me that he penetrated you with the condom on, he ejaculated, took the condom off, and re-entered you?"

"Yeah," Erik responded sheepishly.

"Well, why didn't you just say that in the first place?! Aint no need to lie! I understand that shit happens! I got gonorrhea when I was sixteen, and, obviously, I don't always practice safe sex, because we haven't protected ourselves! I know how it is when you're in the moment! Just learn from this shit, but don't lie!" I said angrily.

I absolutely deplored dishonesty. I could not handle it mentally. My mind went into overdrive from one single lie, no matter how "small" or "big" the lie. Once a lie was told to me, it always led to the eventual demise of the relationship. I could not trust the person. I surmised that, if the person would lie about something miniscule, they would also lie about something that they perceived as significant. I strongly urged each and every one of my past lovers to tell me the truth, whether it would hurt me or not. My mind could handle the truth, even if my heart could not.

~~~~

The "heart" is designed to feel. The mind is designed to think. My foolish heart had convinced my mind to ignore the obvious: there was very little chance that Erik could have Chlamydia for five months and not have passed it on to me, especially when I considered how often we had sex, which was everyday, several times a day for two weeks.

Foolishly, I allowed my heart to do the work of my mind: I forgave Erik for his initial dishonesty, and I remained in the relationship, rather than to run like a bat fleeing from the fiery pits of Hell.

Prior to the truth of Erik's actions being known regarding his contraction of Chlamydia, he told me that he had NEVER had unprotected sex with anyone other than his ex, with whom he was in a committed relationship—all the while, knowing full well that he had unprotected sex with someone other than his ex-partner. And, to make matters worse, while he was claiming not to have EVER had unprotected sex, other than with his ex, he had the audacity to try to make me be ashamed for having had unprotected sex with Marco.

Although Erik's act of dishonesty had already hurled a devastating blow to our infant relationship, more assaults were soon to follow.

"Who were you texting?" I asked Erik as he entered his bedroom from the living room one evening.

"Nobody…just this dude that goes to school with me. He was trying to get me to come over to his house to study…"

"You lying," I said calmly from my vantage on his bed.

"No, I'm not. He asked me if I wanted to study with him…"

"You lying," I repeated calmly, again.

"His name John…He go to Candler…He invited me over to study," he added. Candler was the name of the theological school at Emory.

"You are LYING!" I yelled. I could not take his lies anymore. I generally did not call people liars, nor did I refer to their behavior as lying, but I knew no other word that appropriately expressed my feelings at that moment. "Are you going to tell me what really was said?" I asked angrily.

"I'm telling you what he said."

My heart beat erratically within my chest. Erik was not going to tell the truth, no matter how many times I told him that he was lying. His actions were beyond frightening. I would have thought that at some point he would have conceded, but he maintained his position of deceit.

"I was lying here looking for a movie on your iPad as text messages started to come through. I ignored the first few, because I don't like to invade a person's privacy, but then I saw the words, 'it's too late', and a Voice told me to read the messages. I laid here fighting the urge to read them, until finally I acquiesced. I read all the shit that y'all texted. I read the guy's statement to you in which he expressed that he wanted some yellow cake in reference to your ass; I read where he asked you to come over to watch a movie and eat pizza; and, I read where you laughed at his sexual advances; I read all of it!"

My voice broke as I yelled. I was hurt beyond simple words could accurately articulate. "I can't believe that you would banter with someone in a sexually suggestive manner and I'm in the next fuckin' room, not even twelve feet from you! We had just eaten dinner together, enjoyed each other's company, and, minutes later, you textin' with some nigga about your ass and him wanting you to come to watch a movie and eat muthafuckin' pizza together! That shit take a lot of gotdamn nerve, especially considering, I'm in the next damn room!"

Erik stood motionless as I rose from the bed to put on my clothes. I had never quite felt the kind of pain that I was experiencing. I had been in relationships before where my partners were unfaithful, but their actions did not affect me in the same way that Erik's did. I had placed more trust in Erik; I expected more of him.

~~~

I did not leave Erik's home that night. As I prepared to leave, Erik asked me to give him an opportunity to explain his actions. According to Erik, the guy with whom he texted, had taken and passed a class in which Erik was currently enrolled. Erik was scheduled to take his first examination in the class in a few days. Because the guy had successfully passed the course, Erik asked him for his notes and old tests, from which he could study. The messages that I read between the two of them ensued as a result of Erik's request of the guy's notes and tests.

Erik apologized profusely for his actions, blaming the rigor of his courses as to the reason for his behavior. I did not wholly accept his excuse. I felt that, if he would go to such lengths as to entertain the advances of a guy in order to get a passing grade on a test, there was no way of knowing what else he would do to accomplish his goals.

I should have ended my relationship with Erik that night. Yet, unbeknownst to me, he had already pierced the thick lining surrounding my heart, making a home for himself deep within its chambers. I was embarking upon a roller coaster ride; one that could have very well claimed my life.

"Here's the password to my accounts. You can read whatever you want. I want to earn your trust in me, again," Erik said to me as he knelt down to kiss me before he left for school.

I did not go to work. Instead, I lay in Erik's bed thinking of the predicament in which I was involved. *I needed to get out of the relationship before I became more emotionally attached, I reminded myself.* Yet, rather than to listen to my inner voice, I remained on his bed and hesitatingly clicked on Erik's iPad.

I really had not intended to read any of his text messages. I thought that I would simply look at the blank screen for a moment and then get up from the bed to begin my day. However, a feeling deep within me beckoned to me to read the messages. Just as before when I discovered his text exchanges with his schoolmate, I obliged.

Hours upon hours passed before I stopped reading Erik's messages. I did not know what Erik was thinking when he offered to allow me to read them. Actually, I did know: it was obvious to me that he was not thinking.

I was in shock. The person whom I read about was not the person in whom I had freely given my heart. Text message after text message revealed a dishonest, manipulative, whoremonger—the true person with whom I had fallen dangerously in love.

~~~

My relationship with Erik waged on for several more months. As was the case with the other dysfunctional relationships in which I had been involved, Erik and I had many, many beautiful moments of what appeared to be love; though laced within the façade of love were arguments and more lies.

After having attempted to end the relationship many times, it successfully met its demise during the early spring months of 2015. Despite the turmoil and pain that resulted during the relationship, I grieved its demise in a way that I had not mourned any of my previous romantic relationships.

I had great hope in Erik; in our relationship. I had grown weary of the dysfunction that seemed to accompany every romantic relationship that I entered. I was exhausted.

I had done all that I knew to do in the name of love; yet, the outcome had always been the same. It seemed as though all of my good efforts were in vain; that no matter the amount of good I did, the results always ended in unhealthy, dissatisfying relationships.

~~~~

"Ugh, I remember I used to want to kick his ass!" LaNeeka laughed as she expressed her utter disdain of Erik several weeks after the demise of my relationship with him. I laughed prematurely with her.

"I thought you said that you didn't dislike him?" I asked. My laughter had begun to subside as the totality of her words registered in my mind.

"Well, I…I…I didn't dislike…I mean, I…"

From time to time, I would ask LaNeeka specific questions regarding her feelings toward various things that occurred in her life. Unlike me, she sometimes had difficulty directly expressing her true feelings; though, at times, the truth of her feelings slid from her tongue, like venom from the fangs of a reptile.

"But, you just said that you wanted to kick his ass. If you wanted to kick his ass, you must have disliked him at some point, though, each time that I asked you how you felt about him, you said that you did not harbor ill-feelings toward him."

"I didn't…I mean…I just didn't like some of the things he did," LaNeeka managed to say.

Her words came as much as a surprise to me as did my response came as a surprise to her.

"Yea, but each time that I asked you how you felt about him, you always said something contrary to what you just said now. Erik was right about you…" I said as I pondered the woman whom I had given my love, attention, and care to for the past four years.

Months prior, before Erik and I had officially begun our romantic relationship, I made him aware of my former romantic relationship with LaNeeka, and that we had conceived and aborted our child. After my admission, Erik had openly expressed distrust of LaNeeka.

"I don't trust her. I know women. They'll wait until they have the opportunity and then they'll try something. They're devious."

I laughingly disregarded his statements. I considered his thoughts about LaNeeka's character to be the result of insecurities within himself, which, in turn, caused him to question the validity and the fact that LaNeeka and I actually enjoyed a true friendship, despite having been former romantic partners.

"Naw, you don't know LaNeeka. She's not like that; this girl has one of the sweetest spirits I know. She doesn't have a deceitful, calculating bone in her body."

However, as I sat across from LaNeeka, my opinion began to change as the truth replaced my naiveté. I had known LaNeeka to tell untruths on occasion, though I did not think of her as a dishonest or manipulative person. Yet, as I mentally re-visited some of our verbal exchanges, I wondered if I had been wrong about the person I thought she was.

"Neeka, my daddy and Josephine said that you want to marry me," I stated jokingly into my cellular phone one day.

"Uh-uhn, I don't want you! I love you, but not like that!" LaNeeka insisted.

"Waaaaaaiiiiit a minute! Don't say it like that now; like I ain't nothing but yesterday's news!!!" I laughed heartily.

"No, I don't mean it like that! I'm just saying that I don't want to be with you."

I laughed. "It's cool. I was just messin' with you. It doesn't hurt my feelings or offend me that you're not interested in me anymore."

I wholeheartedly accepted LaNeeka's loss of feelings toward me. I knew that, in some ways, she would always love me, though I was glad that she had healed from the loss of our relationship, and that she valued our friendship in the same manner that I did.

Yet, a few more weeks after the termination of my relationship with Erik, more truths revealed themselves.

"I was thinking about all of the shit that I went through with Erik! I woulda been better off if I had stayed with you, at least I could trust you!" I laughed. "Shoot, we might as well get married and fuck all this foolishness with these niggas in these streets! You want to get married?!" I asked jokingly.

"Yes," LaNeeka replied seriously.

"Huh?? Girl, I was just talkin' mess!" I laughed uneasily. "A couple weeks ago, you just told me, my daddy, and Josephine that you didn't want me. Now, you turning around talking about you want to get married!"

"Hahaha, I was just joking. I don't want to get married to you," LaNeeka said in feigned humor.

"Na, you were serious," I stated in a tone of somberness that replaced the previous humor in my conversation.

For days afterward, I continued to process LaNeeka's words to me.

"Neeka, would you do all for anyone else all that you've done for me?" I asked contemplatively into my cell phone to her, as I lay on the bed in my dad's guest room in Atlanta and she was in Toledo.

"Huh?" LaNeeka asked confusingly.

"Would you have done for someone else the same kind, gracious, and generous things that you've done for me?" Several moments passed without a response from LaNeeka. "I didn't think so," I conceded.

I felt duped. A part of me felt that I should have been honored that LaNeeka had gone to the lengths that she did to achieve my love and devotion; yet, another part of me felt betrayed. I trusted LaNeeka. If asked if there was any living person in whom I trusted most, I would have unhesitatingly chosen LaNeeka.

I understood romantic love very well. I was a hopeless romantic to the core of my being. Aside from my desire to fulfill the Creator's will and to meet my basic needs of sustenance (food, clothing, shelter), I had no greater want than to be in a healthy, loving romantic relationship. Though, despite a great understanding of my wants/needs, I would not have manipulated and lied to anyone in an effort for him/her to be with me.

LaNeeka was far more to me than simply a former lover or a friend; she was my confidant, my Earth-angel, my Geneva.

Having gone through so much in my life and without the divine embodiment of what I believed LaNeeka represented, my will to live faltered. I lost faith in humanity. I felt that, if a truly beautifully-natured person like LaNeeka could behave so selfishly, what could I expect from the rest of the world's inhabitants?

~~~

I quietly lay on the bed in the second bedroom of my daddy's apartment as scenes from my life passed before my mind's eyes: I recalled the sadness in Mama's eyes when I last saw her; I remembered the hurt in Geneva's voice as she related the mean things that had been done to her by those whom she loved most; I saw the hurtful things that I had endured from my parents; a collage of past lovers and friends flashed before me…

*I had no reason or no person for whom to live…*None…At forty-one years of age, I was unemployed, I lived with my father, and I did not have a car…I felt alone in an unyielding world…the persons who were unknowingly the wind beneath my wings had traversed to the land of milk and honey.

I no longer had Allen's rallies, "Aww, come on, Mandingo!"

I was without Mama or Mother's love quietly motivating me to succeed.

Aunt Carol's gentle, assured spirit was not able to guide my steps.

Geneva's soft words of inspiration were deafened.

Death had robbed me. It had taken from me the people whose lives were a beacon of hope for me, silencing their cries of encouragement.

"Tell your story, Chris!" His Voice echoed from decades before.

I shifted positions on the bed, rolling onto my right side. "Tell your story!" His Voice admonished once more.

My nearly defeated mind faltered; hesitated to answer His call. Deep within me, however, my soul quivered.

Vivid visuals of my deceased family members flashed before me. Bathed in light, one by one their spirits greeted me: Allen…Geneva…Mama…Aunt Carol…Mother. Words did not escape their lips, only images of them stood before me as tears streamed from my eyes.

I felt the warm, soothing embrace of their divine love of me. I understood their purposes in my life…the reason for my journey became clear…the obscured became known; forgotten lessons were remembered.

I more fully realized that my life was not my own…I was not placed on Earth for my personal satisfaction; for my vainglory. The divine purpose for which I existed, for which I had been created, seeped into my consciousness. The Holy Spirit tugged at my spirit until I fully understood my purpose on Earth.

I had been chosen for the glorification of God. Through my sufferings, His strength was made known.

Rising from the shackles of despair, I turned on my laptop computer. I needed to share my story. Opening the word document that contained my second autobiography, I worked tirelessly for weeks editing the completed manuscript. Once finished, I quickly dove into the arduous task of writing my third autobiography until its completion.

~~~~

My life was akin to a roller coaster ride: there were times when I experienced the thrills of emotional bliss and the exhilaration of accomplished goals; while, at other times, I begrudgingly waded through the sorrow and misery of death, failed relationships, unemployment, and homelessness.

Over the course of my journey, the Spirit taught me the value of forgiveness and acceptance. It was when I truly embodied forgiveness and acceptance of a person wherever he or she finds himself/herself that the Creator began to allow me to experience the beauty of life.

My life was filled with challenges; moments of deep sadness, struggle, and, at times, strife; yet, within those moments of anguish, Love (God) could still be seen and felt.

The Spirit of God encouraged me to always keep my hand in His; that is, to maintain my focus on Him and His ways, no matter the mayhem that occurred around or within me. In doing so, I found that the hardships of life not only became much easier to bear, but that His spirit could also be seen and felt and heard *In the Midst of It All.*

The End

www.ingramcontent.com/pod-product-compliance
Lightning Source LLC
Chambersburg PA
CBHW052018290426
44112CB00014B/2292